The 2019 Jacob D. Maendel Lectures

Blessings and Burdens
100 Years of Hutterites in Manitoba

IAN KLEINSASSER

© 2019 Ian Kleinsasser

All rights reserved. No part of this publication may be reproduced, stored in a retrieval system, or transmitted in any form or by any means without the prior written permission of the publisher.

Cover Image: *Ältester* Joseph Kleinsasser (Sunnyside, MB) and Jacob Kleinsasser (Crystal Spring, MB), 1974. Joseph Kleinsasser served as elder from 1967 to 1978 and was succeeded by Jacob Kleinsasser who served from 1978 to 2017. Between the two, they led the Schmiedeleut for 50 years. [SOURCE: Jacob Kleinsasser Collection.]

The artistic representation of Jacob D. Maendel used for the Jacob D. Maendel Lectures logo was designed by Brendan Maendel.

ISSN 2562-7481

ISBN 978-1-927913-95-6

Library and Archives Canada Cataloguing in Publication
Title: Blessings and burdens : 100 years of Hutterites in Manitoba / Ian Kleinsasser.
Names: Kleinsasser, Ian, 1976- author.
Description: Series statement: The 2019 Jacob D. Maendel Lectures, 2562-7481 | The inaugural Jacob D. Maendel Lectures were presented at Trinity United Church, Portage la Prairie, MB on June 1 and 8, 2019.
Identifiers: Canadiana 20190165170 | ISBN 9781927913956 (softcover)
Subjects: LCSH: Hutterian Brethren—Manitoba—History.
Classification: LCC BX8129.H8 K54 2019 | DDC 289.7/7127—dc23

Box 40 • MacGregor, MB • R0H 0R0
p. 204-272-5132 • f. 204-252-2381 • e. orders@hbbookcentre.com

Printed in Canada.

The inaugural
Jacob D. Maendel Lectures
were presented at
Trinity United Church, Portage la Prairie, MB
on June 1 and 8, 2019.

TABLE OF CONTENTS

Introduction -- I
Lecture One: Beginnings: Coming to Manitoba --------------------- 1
Lecture Two: "Like the World, Only Later in Time" ------------- 37
Lecture Three: 1974: The "Year of Jubilee" ------------------------- 73
About Jacob D. Maendel --109
About Ian Kleinsasser --- 111

INTRODUCTION

On June 1 and 8, 2019, Hutterites in Manitoba made history. For the first time since settling in the Canadian Prairie Provinces, a Hutterite with an academic background in history interpreted and presented part of the Hutterite story in front of a public audience. The inaugural Jacob D. Maendel Lectures Series was presented by Ian Kleinsasser in three one-hour lectures at Trinity United Church in Portage la Prairie, Manitoba. The audiences ranged from 150–200 and consisted predominantly of Hutterites from Schmiedeleut Group I, but also several members from Schmiedeleut Group II. Numerous Mennonites and other non-Hutterites also participated.

The Jacob D. Maendel Lectures were conceived and planned by an *ad hoc* task force working to commemorate the centennial of permanent Hutterite settlement in Manitoba, Canada. The purpose of the lectures is to bring the academic fields of history, theology, and literature, broadly conceived, under the discipline of, and into the service of the Church. In other words, the scholarship presented is to be of high calibre, but not merely an academic exercise for its own sake. Rather, the scholarship is to have direct ecclesiological implications, in the spirit of the motto, "*Ecclesia semper reformanda est* [the church must always be reformed]." The church can and must learn from the academy and, in turn, offer a witness and a prophetic critique to the academy and the wider world.

In the years to come, the series is expected to stimulate learning and invite discussion about topics of interest to the Hutterite community. The lectures attempt to cultivate something of Jacob D. Maendel's vision for the church; this vision, as we understand it, includes a deep appreciation for Hutterite history and the broader

Ian Kleinsasser delivering the inaugural Jacob D. Maendel lectures on June 8, 2019.
[PHOTO: Sheri Wollmann.]

Christian tradition, an openness to non-Hutterites and new ideas, a reverence for creation, and a boldness in putting convictions into action.

In regard to the 2019 lectures, there are a few observations worth noting. First, lectures like *Blessings and Burdens: 100 Years of Hutterites in Manitoba* are somewhat similar to first-year university courses; in the process of painting the big picture, they sacrifice detail and nuance. This obvious shortcoming is mitigated by the usefulness of having the overarching narrative sketched out and presented in a logical way with essential facts and historical turning points carefully identified. The lectures presented here in published form will provide a useful outline for the experience of Hutterites in Manitoba from which more detailed historical analysis can proceed. Indeed, in numerous respects, Kleinsasser's work represents a cautious 'first word' on this era in Hutterite history.

It is a basic fact that all history writing has biases. Good history writing, however, attempts to be open and honest about the biases the author brings to the task. Regarding the work of Ian Kleinsasser found within these pages, there are at least three shaping factors to note: First, he is the nephew of the late *Ältester* Jacob Kleinsasser under whose leadership the 1992 Schism of the Schmiedeleut Conference occurred; this relatively recent history is still highly charged for all parties involved. In the pursuit of transparency, Kleinsasser worked closely with various non-Schmiedeleut Group I scholars to ensure a fair and charitable treatment of the conflict. Secondly, he has had the benefit of access to the many unpublished sources found in the archival collection amassed by Jacob Kleinsasser during his lengthy and productive tenure as *Ältester*. Many of these original documents are in German and have been translated for these lectures, providing an immediacy and richness to the narrative. Finally, readers will notice that the lectures occasionally utilize language from the Hutterite vernacular which may pose a challenge for non-Hutterite readers. Given the time constraints Kleinsasser had to cope with—100 years in three hours—this was a useful shorthand.

We are grateful to have benefited from the careful and thoughtful scholarship of Ian Kleinsasser; the work he has done in crafting and weaving a narrative of one hundred years of blessings and burdens the Hutterite church has experienced in Manitoba, Canada, will serve as a useful framework for further historical inquiry into the Hutterianism of the 20th-century. It appears obvious to us that releasing *Blessings and Burdens: 100 Years of Hutterites in Manitoba* in published form will be of benefit both to the academy and the church for years to come.

Kenny Wollmann & Jesse Hofer
July 2019

LECTURE ONE
Beginnings: Coming to Manitoba

The first portion of this three-part series focuses on the years between 1918 and 1930. I will briefly explore the impetus for immigration to Canada by looking at some of the key factors which caused the Hutterites to leave South Dakota and move to Canada. I will then look at the actual settlement process in Manitoba. For this section, I am drawing almost exclusively on the ground-breaking research of local historian, Bruce Wiebe. I not only want to acknowledge his amazing work, but also take this opportunity to thank him for the dedication he has shown to the history of our people. Indeed, Bruce is a direct descendant of Prairieleut Hutterites and Mennonites.

We will also explore some of the discrimination faced by the Hutterites, such as the 1919 Order in Council or Hutterite ban, which stopped Hutterite migration into Canada, as well as discrimination and changes in the Hutterite education system which, in Victor Peters' words, "has penetrated Hutterian society most powerfully."[1] Our last major topic in lecture one will explore the early history of the Bruderhof and how they made contact with Hutterites in North America. To conclude, we will explore some of the important challenges that arose because of the Hutterite/Bruderhof relationship as well as reflect on the significance of these lectures.

The Back-Story: Impetus for Migration to Canada

So why are we here in Manitoba? An unknown Hutterite chronicler gives us the *Coles Notes* version:

---

1   Victor Peters, *All Things Common: the Hutterian Way of Life* (Minneapolis: University of Minnesota Press, 1965), 137.

The first thing you want to remember is that the emigration from South Dakota to Canada was caused by the war which took place in the year 1914. This war was known as the First World War, and it caused the dear communities [*Gemeinde*] much conflict and sorrow.[2]

For this lecture, I cannot give an exhaustive account of 'what happened.' However, I will try to outline some of the significant factors which ultimately contributed to the Hutterites leaving South Dakota and settling in Canada.

World War I and Anti-German Sentiment

When America entered WWI on April 6, 1917, there were 17 Hutterite communities in South Dakota.[3] For the most part, these German-speaking people lived in prosperous, self-sufficient communities which took care of all the needs of their members, including education. Most of the Hutterite communities still had their teachers who taught in both the German and English languages. Up until April 6, the Hutterites had been well tolerated by their local states and neighbours. Local newspapers referred to the Hutterites as "honest, frugal, industrious and wonderfully law-abiding."[4] A farmer living next to the Rockport community stated, "The Hutterians are a good, honest, reliable, people who will do anything to help a friend."[5] In her report, *The Mennonites* [sic][6] *in South Dakota*, Gertrude S. Young states,

> It would not be possible, I think, to find among a group of foreign contributors to our State greater generosity, finer courtesy and more real kindness. Even among the Hutterians, narrow perhaps, failing maybe in their duties to the world, there is a

---

2   "*Einleitungs-Dokument für die ersten Weltkrieg Dokumenten* [Introductory Document for World War I Document]," n.d., in author's collection.
3   There were a total of 19 communities in the United States at this time, counting the two in Montana. The estimated population was 2000. See John A. Hostetler, *Hutterite Society* (Baltimore: John Hopkins University Press, 1974), 126.
4   A. N. Westhorpe, *Sioux City Tribune*, July 19, 1919.
5   Ole Asklason, *Brookings Register*, April 9, 1920.
6   At this time, Hutterites were commonly confused with Mennonites.

gentleness, humility, and charity of the Man of Galilee.⁷

This all changed in 1917 when the Americans entered the war. Writing in 1920, Bertha Clark notes a dramatic shift in attitude:

> [The Hutterites] have been so quiet and unobtrusive that we were not aware of their presence until, during the war, they were brought before the courts, fined, imprisoned, and at last, by these things, forced to begin upon another exile.⁸

Overnight, neighbours and public opinion turned against the Hutterites because of their refusal to pay war taxes, buy war bonds, or send their boys to fight in the war. They were labelled as "yellow foreigners" and "traitors to God and country." The young men who arrived in the war camps and declared their pacifist stance reported that "the pent-up hatred, the intolerance, and the mass hysteria broke out like a whirlwind."⁹

Conscientious Objection

On the 15th of September, 1917, four Hutterites—two from Rosedale community and two from Tschetter community—received notice to report to the Junction City Training Camp in Kansas. This was just the beginning. In total, 55 Hutterite men made their way to war camps. In the meantime, Hutterite leaders travelled to Washington where they petitioned President Woodrow Wilson and his war secretary, Newton Baker, on behalf of the Hutterite conscientious objectors. While the slow, bureaucratic machinery worked on a solution, the various COs in the camps across the US faced a variety of abuses. One of the most well-known cases of abuse was that of the Hofer brothers, who were court-martialed and sentenced to life imprisonment on Alcatraz. After suffering weeks of abuse, which included high-cuffing and solitary confine-

---

7   State Department of History, *South Dakota Historical Collections*, Vol. 10 (Pierre: Hipple Printing Company, 1920), 506.
8   Bertha W. Clark, "Turners of the Other Cheek," *Survey* 47 (December 31, 1921): 519.
9   A. J. Friedrich Zieglschmid, ed. *Das Klein-Geschichtsbuch der Hutterischen Brüder* (Philadelphia: The Carl Schurz Memorial Foundation, 1947), 477.

ment, the four Hutterites were shipped to Leavenworth Penitentiary in Kansas where two brothers, Michael and Joseph Hofer, died. Without a doubt, this event reawakened memories of past martyrdom and was one of the decisive factors which triggered the migration to Canada.[10]

Abuse at Home

While the Hutterite conscientious objectors faced violence in the war camps, the communities in South Dakota also faced heavy censorship and mistreatment of their own. On the 19th of February, the *Bismarck Evening Tribune* reported that a Hutterite mill had been shut down because ground-up glass was found in their flour.[11] On the 5th of May, the same newspaper reported livestock being 'taken' from the Jamesville community by "patriotic citizens" and sold in lieu of war bonds.[12]

Constitutional Attack

One of the most significant attacks brought against the Hutterites in South Dakota was legal action levelled by the State Council of Defence. Ever since 1905, the Schmiedeleut Hutterites in South Dakota had existed as a unified body incorporated under the name, Hutterische Brüder Gemeinde.[13] The listed purpose of the corporation was:

> promoting, engaging in, and carrying on the Christian religion, Christian worship, and religious education and teachings, according to our religious belief that all members should act together as one being, and have, hold, use, possess, and enjoy all things in common.[14]

---

10 See Duane C. S. Stoltzfus, P*acifists in Chains: The Persecution of Hutterites during the Great War* (Baltimore: John Hopkins University Press, 2013).
11 "Mennonite Mill Grinding Glass." *Bismarck Evening Tribune*, February 19, 1918, 8.
12 "Take Livestock of Mennonites for War Bonds." *Bismarck Evening Tribune*, May 5, 1918.
13 There were, in fact, three corporations: the Hutterische Bruder Gemeinde, the Hutterische Society of Wolf Creek, and the Hutterische Gemeinde of Elm Springs.
14 *Klein-Geschichtsbuch*, 614.

Hoping to destroy the communal system, the State Council for Defense persuaded the state attorney general to use legal action to revoke the 1905 articles of incorporation. The state argued that the Hutterite corporation, instead of serving religious purposes as called for in the charter, was really only used for economic gain and that the Hutterites had amassed a fortune without dedicating any of it to the worship of God. Hutterites, they pointed out, did not even have a church building. They were further described as a menace to society, depriving children of the right to attend county fairs and mingle with the outside world, and punishing members who contributed to the war effort. Although the lengthy legal proceedings finally resulted in a technical annulment of the Hutterite corporation, the Hutterites were allowed to hold their properties as an unincorporated organization. The court did not demand receivership or the liquidation of Hutterite assets requested by the State Council of Defence, but the message had been sent: Hutterites were not welcome in South Dakota because of their insistence to hold on to their pacifist views.[15]

Das Klein-Geschichtsbuch der Hutterischen Brüder, an internal chronicle, states that these combined assaults eventually

> shattered the proverbial overly strained bow of Hutterite forbearance, causing most Hutterite

---

15 Hostetler, *Hutterite Society*, 131.

"Patriotic citizens" confiscated sheep from the Hutterites and sold them to buy Liberty Bonds. Hutterites later donated the proceeds, which they regarded as "blood money," to the Red Cross. [SOURCE: *Yankton Press and Dakotan*, May 4, 1918.]

communities to look for new homes and sell their lands at a loss.[16]

As a parting shot, the South Dakota State Council for Defense insisted that five per cent of the selling price of the land be invested in war bonds and half a per cent be given to the Red Cross. The Hutterites lowered their asking price by the required amount but left the responsibility for purchasing bonds with the buyers.

The Exodus

Precisely when Hutterites first seriously undertook the process of investigating a possible move to Canada is not clear. We do know that inquiries were already made as early as October of 1917. In addition, the Dariusleut settlement at Dominion City, MB, in 1899 played an essential role in laying the groundwork for the pending migration. Of particular importance were the negotiations in 1899 that assured Hutterites the same exemption from military service granted to the Mennonites in 1873.

By late January 1918, three Hutterite representatives met with Commissioner of Immigration J. B. Walker and with the Manitoba Minister of Agriculture and Immigration, Valentine Winkler, in Winnipeg to discuss the move to Canada. The three representatives were Lehrerleut *Ältester* David Hofer, Dariusleut *Ältester* Elias Walter and the secretary of the Hutterische Brüder Gemeinde, Joseph Kleinsasser. This group made inquiries about moving to Saskatchewan and Alberta and asked whether the 1873 military service exemption originally granted to the Mennonites and later to the Hutterites was still valid. By May, the Hutterites appeared satisfied as to their exemption status in Canada but still questioned whether their young men might not yet be subject to the United States Draft to which Superintendent of Immigration W. D. Scott responded that this latter point was unclear, but he reassured them that they were not subject to military service in Canada.[17]

Back in South Dakota, the Schmiedeleut leaders convened a meeting at which they appointed Michael Waldner of Bon Homme,

---

16   *Klein-Geschichtsbuch*, 487.
17   W. Scott to Johnstone, 18 May 1918, Library and Archives Canada (RG 76, Volume 173, File 58764, Part 2).

Paul Gross of Rosedale, and steward Paul Wollman of Huron to travel to Canada to search for land. The group left on the 19th of April taking with them five draft-age young men for whom they intended to find employment during their search for land. The reason for taking the young men was two-fold: one, to get them out of the United States so that they would not be drafted into the military; and two, so that they could earn money to help offset the cost of the move to Canada. Waldner, Gross, and Wollman spent the better part of the month travelling across southern Alberta examining the many properties for sale. Other Hutterite delegates eventually joined them, but both groups came up empty-handed. By May 31 they arrived back in South Dakota.

On June 5, 1918, the Schmiedeleut leaders convened another meeting where they appointed six brothers, one from each community,[18] to travel to Canada to purchase land. After several unsuccessful forays, the group returned to Winnipeg where a local land agent convinced them to look at property in the R. M. of Cartier and the eastern portion of the R. M. of Portage la Prairie. Upon visiting the three properties of 6,000, 3,040, and 9,600 acres respectively, the six delegates decided to purchase one of the properties and secure an option on the others. This initial purchase of 18,640 acres was later added to by subsequent purchases.[19]

Hutterische Brüder Gemeinde Corporation and Land Purchases

Ever since 1905–6, the Hutterische Brüder Gemeinde Corporation, which had purchased all the land for the corporation, was also the registered owner of all South Dakota Schmiedeleut lands. Accordingly, the sales of these lands in 1918 was made under the signatures of its corporate officers and seal. This created, in effect, one communal pool of monies which was then used to finance all the initial Manitoba land purchases which totalled $1,183,309[20]

---

18   Huron actually sent two, while Maxwell sent none. One possible explanation for this is the fact that their minister, Joseph Wipf, had recently passed away.
19   All of the initial purchases involved four land speculators and intermediaries: the Americans, Joseph Malcom Hackney, Alvin Solberg, and Fred Delos McCartney, and Manitoba Senator, Aimé Bénard.
20   With inflation, this is approximately $26 million in 2019.

for ca. 24,279 acres. Interestingly, these initial purchases were not made by individual communities or leaders but were all made by the six brothers initially appointed to this task at the June 5th meeting in South Dakota.[21]

According to the testimony of Joseph Kleinsasser, given at the Fredrick Waldner trial in 1919, the Corporation itself was not continued in Canada as the Schmiedeleut first needed to see whether Canadian law allowed such a corporation to function.[22] Matters were further complicated by the fact that some of the leading members of the Hutterische Brüder Gemeinde Corporation had to stay behind in South Dakota to finalize the land sales, and also to deal with the legal challenges brought against the corporation by the South Dakota State Council for Defense and two Schmiedeleut members who had filed suit against the corporation.

Even though the initial public response to the land sales to the Hutterites was positive, it soon gave way to discontentment and downright hostility. A July 11th issue of the *Oakville Daily Standard* set an upbeat tone when it first broke the news of the Hutterite purchase. These settlers were rumoured to be quite wealthy and would, possibly, stimulate economic growth in the area. By late July and particularly in August of 1918, a large influx of Hutterites arrived in Manitoba to help with the building projects and to harvest the standing crop which had been included in the purchase of

---

21 The six men in whose names this and all other land purchases before March 1921 were registered, constituted a "Holding Committee" for the real estate of the communities. They functioned as "the trustees for the Hutterian Brethren of the Province of Manitoba and who are the owners as trustees, of the real and personal property of the said Hutterian Brethren of the Province of Manitoba." Their names, as recorded on the documents, were: David Hofer, Sr., Paul Wollman, Zacharias Hofer, David Hofer, Jr., Joseph Michel Waldner, and Joseph Waldner. Collectively, on behalf of all Schmiedeleut, they purchased and took title to all lands, entered into Agreements to Purchase, registered Caveats, and assumed liabilities through the purchase of mortgaged properties or themselves mortgaged them to others. In an expression of community, the Schmiedeleut enabled the move for all by choosing to immigrate to Canada as one.

22 On June 1921, the Schmiedeleut adopted "Articles of Association of the Hutterian Brethren" and formed themselves into groups of communities being unincorporated associations. An unincorporated association does not have limited liability; clubs and charities were often constituted as unincorporated associations. The members of a management committee of a charity that is formed as an unincorporated association are likely to be charity trustees.

The farmyard purchased by the Hutterites from Joseph Hackney in 1918. Photo by L. B. Foote, 1916. [SOURCE: Benard Farm 1916, L. B. Foote fonds, P7392/1, Foote.9, Archives of Manitoba.]

the Hackney farm. The entry of these German-speaking pacifists while the country was still at war in Europe, and their acquisition of lands that some thought should be made available for returning soldiers, caused an almost immediate backlash. Much of this opposition came from the Winnipeg Great War Veterans' Association who took it upon themselves to force the Canadian government to enact a Hutterite ban. The situation became quite dangerous as the Veterans' Association threatened to take matters into their own hands to stop any further Hutterites from crossing the Canadian border.

By May 2, 1919, the hostility against the Hutterites reached a fever pitch, and the Canadian government was pressured into passing an Order in Council which banned Hutterites, Mennonites, and Doukhobors from entering into Canada. For the duration of the ban, those persons not yet in Canada were forced to remain in South Dakota, where all but Bon Homme and part of Milltown's lands east of the James River had been sold.[23] In a letter written on the 29th of September 1919, *Ältester* Joseph Kleinsasser explained why the Hutterites had not all moved to Canada at the same time:

> The reason why we did not all at once leave for Canada was twofold. First, because we could not dispose of all our large properties, both real and personal[24] in so short a time, although it was of-

---

23 Refers only to Schmiedeleut and their known lands. The Dariusleut appear to have been incorporated as "Hutterische Society" and the Lehrerleut as "Hutterische Gemeinde." *Citizen-Republican*, September 19, 1918.
24 Prior to this move, the members possessed 19 large farms, thousands of sheep,

Huron Community, Manitoba. As families arrived from South Dakota, they were assigned a stall in this barn where they stayed until communal dwellings were ready.
[SOURCE: Ward Photo Collection and in the HBBC Digital Collection.]

fered for only about one-half of its actual worth. And, secondly, because quite a few of our young men were in camps, and some of them in prison, for refusing to assume military services and nearly all of these young men were married and had families. And as these families were of the same faith with us, we could not sell all of our places and leave these without a home. And we could not abandon these women and children and go to a far-off country.[25]

The Order in Council was only rescinded on June 2, 1922.

Despite this backlash and the passing of the Order in Council, the Schmiedeleut continued with their land purchases and the six South Dakota communities were re-established in Manitoba under the same names: Milltown, Huron, Bon Homme, James Valley, Rosedale, and Maxwell. Shortly thereafter, two more communities were established by these Manitoba communities: Iberville in 1919 by Rosedale and Barrickman in 1920 by Maxwell.

---

cattle, horses and hogs, nine grist mills, and all kinds of farm machinery necessary to operate the large farms.

25 Joseph J. Kleinsasser to "Minister of Immigration and Colonization," 29 September 1919, in author's collection.

Political cartoon portraying the arrival of Hutterites—here confused with Mennonites—in Canada. Published in the September 21, 1918 edition of the *Calgary Eye Opener*, 4.

Until the 24th of March, 1921, all land transactions were dealt with by the Holding Committee on behalf of all the communities. After March 24th, the Holding Committee transferred the commonly held properties to the eight individual communities. Certificates of Title were registered in the names of three trustees for each community. From this point onwards, any new land purchases were made by those particular trustees for each community. One final point of interest is the fact that even though the Schmiedeleut did not have one communal purse among their communities, they did, in this instance, pool all their money to finance the original land purchases.

Impact of the Great Depression

The worldwide Great Depression of the early 1930s also affected Canada and the Hutterite communities. Wheat prices reached new lows, and land values dropped which impacted the Hutterites' debt-servicing ability and eroded the equity in their land. However, internal population growth continued, and the need to establish new communities became a pressing issue for the Schmiedeleut. Three communities established by the Schmiedeleut during this period had to be dissolved because they could not pay off their significant debt. Barrickman established the first of these communities, Gracevale, in 1932 near Teulon, Manitoba. Titles to this property were registered in the name of the Harris Abattoir Company (later known as Canada Packers). Gracevale never owned the land, and the community was liquidated in 1936. An auction sale held at the farm on March 21st of that year disposed of the livestock and machinery.

Similarly, in 1932, Maxwell community established Sundale community on the large Andrew Anderson property in Alberta known as Vogelvik Farm. Sundale, or Alsask as it was most popularly called, would, upon payment over time of $51,200, acquire the farm assets including 2,560 acres. An additional 4,345 acres of land was leased from Anderson with the option to purchase. Noteworthy is that only $1 was paid to Anderson at the time of execution of the documents, and that specified annual payment amounts were based upon the dollar value of the wheat crop grown on lands that had been summer-fallowed the previous year. No doubt such arrangements were based upon the prevailing adverse financial and climatic conditions during the Great Depression. Even though the Hutterites had an excellent reputation as farmers, they were no match for the decade of drought known as the Dirty Thirties and no payments on principal could be made. By mutual agreement, the sale agreement and lease were cancelled in January 1935 and a new lease for one year was entered into, whereby Sundale would pay Anderson one-third share of the 1935 crop. After that, Sundale ceased to exist.

The third community in question, Thorndale (also known as Sharpe), was established when Huron community arranged a five-year lease with option-to-purchase for 2,660 acres south of Manitou, Manitoba from Canadian Senator William Sharpe. Ultimately, Thorndale was not viable, and the community relocated south of Roseisle, Manitoba in 1929 where they purchased a total of 1,920 acres for $49,920. Unfortunately, the Roseisle community was also not financially viable, and its assets were liquidated by

The original Andrew Anderson homestead dwelling on the Vogelvik Farm. This was the basis for Sundale community, commonly called Alsask, established in Alberta by Maxwell in 1932. [SOURCE: Mary Wipf (Sioux Falls, SD).]

an October 1938 Winding-Up Order made by the court, and the property was transferred to the Prudential Insurance Company. After refinancing the debt, the other ten Schmiedeleut communities assumed responsibility for the repayment of an equal portion of the remainder. The interest of 6% on each community's subsequent $4,300 debt was to be reduced to 5% if such community marketed its grain through the North West Commission Company.

Of particular interest is the fact that even though Schmiedeleut communities had incorporated as individual communities in 1931 as a protection against indebtedness, they continued to provide financial aid to each other. Current research has not been able to determine whether debts absorbed by the Schmiedeleut collective were ever repaid or were simply reckoned as losses for the communities making the payments—in other words, viewed by all as part of the overall cost of immigration to Canada.

Articles of Association: Unincorporated to Incorporation

Shortly after establishing themselves in Manitoba, the Schmiedeleut adopted the Articles of Association of the Hutterian Brethren (June 1921) and formed themselves into groups of communities being unincorporated associations. Today, clubs and charities are often constituted as unincorporated associations. Based on oral tradition, the unincorporated association model was a good fit for the early Schmiedeleut communities as the communities did not generate enough money to show a profit. However, as the communities became more established and began paying off their debts, some of the communities started to record end-of-year profits, and thus the association had to start paying income tax (covered in our last lecture). Again, according to oral tradition, this situation was further complicated when one of the Associate communities, Barrickman, ran into financial difficulty with a loan they had taken out with Great-West Life Insurance. As the Schmiedeleut were all members of one unincorporated association, Great-West Life Insurance went after the other communities to recover their money. The two wealthier communities at the time were Rosedale and Blumengart. How much money Rosedale had to pay is unknown, but Blumengart ended up paying $10,000 to appease the insurance company.

Mainly because of these two factors, the Schmiedeleut communities changed their legal structure. On the 27th of February 1931, all baptized members of the individual Schmiedeleut communities signed a Memorandums of Agreement acknowledging the pending incorporation and that all real and personal property then held in trust for that particular community would become the property of the newly incorporated entity. At the same time, the Memorandum of Agreement listed joint debts which would have to be distributed equally among the Schmiedeleut communities, should the association ever be dissolved.[26] What this Memorandum of Agreement was referring to was a joint collective debt owed by the Schmiedeleut to the Molson Bank. This 'communal' obligation can be further seen in the actual wording of the 1931 Articles of Incorporation which state: "The corporation assumed and are liable for all indebtedness of the said Hutterian Brethren Church to the Bank of Montreal as at [sic] April 20, 1931."[27] On the 20th

---

26 "Memorandum of Agreement," February 27, 1931, in the author's collection. See also Bruce Wiebe, "Hutterite Immigration to Manitoba: The Land Transactions," in *Navigating Tradition and Innovation*.
27 "The Barickman Hutterian Mutual Corporation Incorporation Act," April 20, 1931, point 6: "Liability for debts."

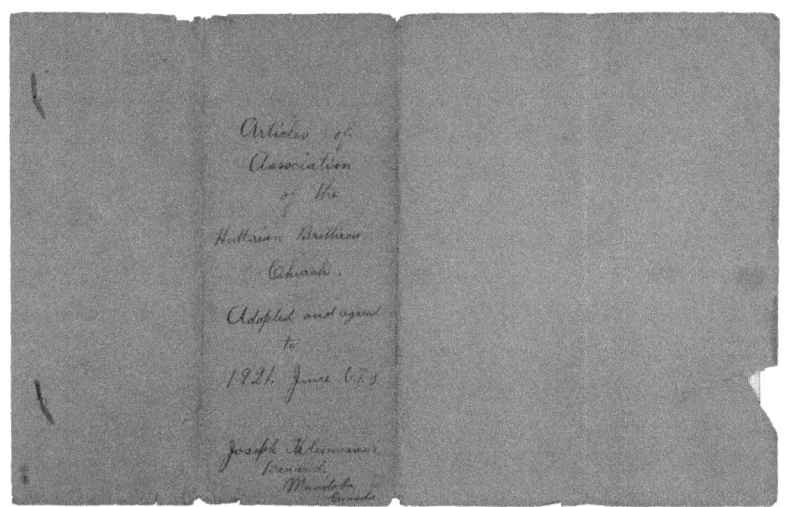

Cover of Joseph Kleinsasser's copy of the 1921 Articles of Association of the Hutterian Brethren Church. [SOURCE: Author's collection.]

of April, 1931 the ten existing Hutterite communities—Barrickman, Blumengart, Bon Homme, Huron, Iberville, James Valley, Maxwell, Milltown, Rosedale, and Roseisle—each incorporated as mutual corporations.

A complete picture of the financial situation facing the Schmiedeleut transition from South Dakota to Manitoba is outside the scope of this lecture. To say that the costs of this migration were considerable would be a gross understatement. Land speculators like Hackney and McCartney realized huge profits as they quickly bought up land and resold it to the Hutterites at, in some cases, an astounding 210% profit.[28] The effects of this profiteering by land speculators was exacerbated by the fact that the Schmiedeleut had sold their lands in South Dakota for less than half its value. This amounted to a severe debt load which took the Schmiedeleut many years to repay. In the Bruderhof publication, *Brothers Unite*, there is an intriguing reference to what must be the beginning of the practise, among some *Leut*, of having the menfolk leave the community to find employment during the winter months. Eberhard Arnold writes,

---

28 Bruce Wiebe, "Hutterite Immigration to Manitoba: The Land Transactions" in *Navigating Tradition and Innovation* (MacGregor: Hutterian Brethren Book Centre, forthcoming).

>The *Hofs* in debt try to help themselves by sending their ablest men outside by twos or twenties in the autumn and winter to take on harvesting or smithy work or the like. All money earned is at once sent home to the steward.[29]

In summary, the early years of the Schmiedeleut in Canada can be characterized by great hardships as they faced the harsh Manitoba winters, manoeuvred around unscrupulous land speculators, and struggled with the ever-evolving legal and spiritual dimensions of the Schmiedeleut Church. Indeed, the Hutterite Church, in general, was constantly shaped by the changing social, legal, and financial systems of their host nation.

In the post-World War I era, the anti-immigrant rhetoric directed at the Hutterites earlier faded away. Newspaper articles were now referring to Hutterites as first-class farmers of which more were needed. The same newspapers called for the repeal of the Order in Council or Hutterite ban. In articles written after WWI, arguments had been made that the Hutterites' settlement patterns were interfering with the development of particular municipalities by more desirable settlers. Now, they took a swing at the land speculators, noting that the main reason Hutterites settled in Manitoba was "to enable certain land speculators to get out from under with a good profit on their transaction" and in this there was "evidence obtainable of the complicity of men high in the public life of Canada."[30] From the documented land transactions it is clear that the availability of large plots of land was initially due to American speculators Joseph Hackney and Fred McCartney, and subsequently to Manitobans Aimé Bénard,[31] John Flanders,[32] and Portage la

---

29 *Brothers Unite: An Account of the Uniting of Eberhard Arnold and the Rhön Bruderhof with the Hutterian Church* (Rifton: Plough Publishing House, 1988), 140.
30 *Winnipeg Free Press*, April 16, 1919, 9.
31 He held positions as a financial agent, vice president of the Standard Supply and Investment Company, and the Franco Canadienne Investment Company. He farmed 4,000 to 5,000 acres at Benard and maintained a dairy farm of 300 purebred cows. He also ranched 1,000 cattle at Lake Winnipeg. In 1907, he was elected to the Manitoba Legislature and resigned in September 1917 when appointed to the senate.
32 He was a director of the Monarch Life Assurance Company and supervisor of the mortgage department of the Sun Life Assurance Company.

Prairie Real Estate Brokers Charles Burley and Joseph Metcalfe, in addition to others.

In contrast to these American speculators who were out to make a quick dollar, the Hutterites were here to establish a permanent Canadian presence but paid a steep price. They took over ownership from the Canadian speculators as well and worked to preserve the land for their children. As a communal society, they eliminated the need for the property to change ownership each succeeding generation. With forbearance and forgiveness, they countered greed, deception, cronyism, misunderstanding, and animosity. The 1890s Prairieleut and Dariusleut settlement attempts were unsuccessful, but 2018 will mark the centennial of the Schmiedeleut in Manitoba. One measure of their success is evident on a property ownership map where the first nine communities to establish themselves in Manitoba, still exist today.[33]

Education

Very early in our history, Hutterite leaders recognized the importance of education to the spiritual development of a child. Early educational pioneers like Hieronymus Käls, Peter Riedemann, and later Peter Walpot are credited with establishing and drafting the initial guidelines for Hutterite schools. These leaders looked at their Reformation era society and recognized ignorance and illiteracy as a limiting and destructive force. They established schools where both boys and girls learned to read because they felt that every person, regardless of their gender, should be able to read the Bible and have the opportunity to be transformed by the Gospel.

Over the years, Hutterites have tried to model their schools according to these early patterns with varying degrees of success because we have no clear picture of what education in the 16th-century actually looked like. For instance, in Russia, the lack of education was a substantial factor that led to the decline in community-of-goods.

---

33 Bruce Wiebe, "Hutterite Immigration to Manitoba."

When community-of-goods was re-established in the Molotschna, the Hutterites immediately sent young men to the Mennonite teacher training school in Halbstadt. Later, when the Hutterites immigrated to the United States, they again saw the importance of education and sent nine men to acquire their teaching certificates.

Settlement in South Dakota, however, represents a significant shift being introduced into the Hutterite school system. In Europe, the Hutterites had total control of their children's education. The threat of losing this control had been the impetus for at least two previous migrations. The settlement years in South Dakota were, by all accounts, difficult years as the Hutterite communities struggled to build up their communities in a pioneering environment, while at the same time attempting to define what community life should look like. Possibly for this reason, Hutterites grudgingly allowed non-Hutterite teachers to teach alongside their own educators. A citation from Bertha Clark's paper captures some of the concerns surrounding education in the New World: "English is taught most willingly in all the schools. The thing that is feared is the way it is taught and the one who may be sent from outside to teach it."[34]

What Bertha Clark meant with "the way it is taught" is unclear, but a reference from the *South Dakota Historical Collections* may give further insight. The paper states:

> The [Hutterite] children are instructed in religious matters during summer schools or sessions after school hours, but their grade instruction is received in the public schools....[35]

Here we see that religious instruction was delegated to "during summer school" and "after school hours." For the majority of the day, the students were instructed by either Hutterite or non-Hutterite educators using the state curriculum.

When the Hutterites migrated to Canada in 1918, this model underwent a dramatic change. Canadian officials had considerable experience with diverse ethnic and religious groups. Earlier Men-

---

34 Bertha W. Clark, "'The Huterisch People': A View from the 1920s," edited by Clifton H. Jones, *South Dakota History* 7, No. 1 (Winter 1976): 9.
35 *South Dakota Historical Collections*, Vol. 10, 503.

Rosedale, Manitoba School Children, date unknown.
[SOURCE: Jacob Kleinsasser Photo Collection]

nonite migrations, Icelandic communities established along the shores of Lake Winnipeg, Mormons and large groups of Ukrainians all had to be accommodated. Many of these groups had struggled to accept Canadian educational requirements. Since Manitoba struggled to introduce the public school in different ethnic areas, the press noted with satisfaction that the Hutterites were prepared to accept the public school without a murmur of protest. A *Winnipeg Free Press* article states,

> The Hutterites, although a German sect, differ from the Mennonites in one important regard. They are not opposed to the school laws of the country in which they live, and while in the United States have never caused trouble such as the Mennonites have occasioned in Manitoba.[36]

The question that we have to struggle with today is why our forebears allowed the public education system to take over the education of their children entirely "without a murmur of protest." Education, after all, is one of the main vehicles of acculturation and assimilation. Has the public school system served us well in cultivating vibrant faith communities? Victor Peters observed that

> although the Hutterians feel that the public school will adversely affect the future of their community, consistent with their doctrine of nonresistance,

---

36 *Winnipeg Free Press*, December 15, 1922.

they have at no time challenged the position of the imposed instruction.[37]

This is an intriguing explanation, but one that I find unsatisfactory. Our foreparents had, on at least two occasions in their history, abandoned their homes and moved to another country because they refused to allow non-Hutterites to educate their children. Even in the United States and Canada, some Hutterite leaders strongly voiced their objections to these compromises. In a letter written to Michael Waldner of Bon Homme, SD, Johann Entz laments:

> It appears that our efforts to remove the Englanders from our schools will not work. This is a sourdough that we should attempt to sweep out as soon as possible. Will such a person be able to instill in our children the proper foundation for communal living? What would our forefathers have done if they had been compelled to allow a worldly man to teach their children?[38]

Similarly, Dariusleut *Ältester* Joseph Stahl wrote,

> Here it is awful, and in Canada even worse, since most communities do not have their teachers for teaching English, and therefore are forced to use teachers from the outside. This means that for eight to ten months a year our children are under the influence of a warlike, worldly education, which cannot do any good; and we are very aware it is leading to corruption. May God be gracious to us.[39]

I do not intend to discount the exceptional work of non-Hutterite educators in Hutterite schools of the past and today, but as a society, we must ask ourselves whether we have a vision of what our schools should be and whether we are really assuming responsibility for the education of our children.

---

37   Victor Peters, *All Things Common*, 138.
38   Johann Entz to Michael Waldner, "*Wegen Englische Lehrer in Der Schule* [Regarding non-Hutterite teachers in the Schools]," 17 Aug. 1925, in author's collection.
39   Jerald Hiebert, *The Hutterite Story of a Pure Church: a Study of Dariusleut Alberta Hutterites, 1918–2000* (Master's Thesis, Regent College 2001), 86.

Despite these objections, the Hutterites in Canada allowed the public school to take partial control of their children's education. This allowed the process of what Victor Peters referred to as "social disorganization" to take root.[40] Later, Peters tempers this criticism by observing that,

> In most cases the officials of the Department of Education have resisted the temptation to use the schools deliberately for disruption of colony life. Instead, they maintain that the primary objective of the public school is to raise the existing standards in all grades and extend general interest in education beyond the grade school level.[41]

"The Hutterites," Peters writes,

> had reached a compromise with the public school system. As long as the public school was located on the colony under the watchful eyes of the community people, they did not object to it, or the learning of English in school.[42]

Thus, over time, we see a gradual erosion of Hutterite control over the education of their children.[43] Hutterite educators were effectively removed from the classroom, and religious and German instruction had to happen outside of the regular school day. Thus, a

40   Victor Peters, *All Things Common*, 137.
41   Ibid., 140.
42   Ibid., 49.
43   The influx of Hutterite students into the various municipalities meant that the school districts were too small to accommodate all the students. At the same time, the Department of Education, largely under the influence of Dr. Robert Fletcher, formed the Hutterian landholdings into school districts. Hutterite communities were required to provide the school building and, in many cases, a teacherage. Whereas in South Dakota both Hutterites and non-Hutterite teachers instructed Hutterite students, in Canada the officials made it clear that only fully qualified English-speaking teachers were allowed to teach in the schools. Hutterites could not elect their own school board for two reasons: 1. According to the Manitoba School Act, school trustees must be born or naturalized Canadians. The Hutterites were American citizens. 2. Elected school trustees must be registered and resident landowners. Because the Hutterites are not individually registered property owners, they do not qualify for the office of school trustees. In later years, once Hutterites acquired Canadian citizenship, they did serve as school trustees. However, for some reason, school trustees had to have their picture taken. Hutterites objected strongly to his requirement but ultimately had to give in.

compromise begun in South Dakota became the accepted practise in Manitoba. Should we today not view this as a total abdication of our responsibility towards our children and our future? One of the harshest Hutterite critics, who lamented what he saw happening in the Hutterite schools, was Hans Decker from Wolf Creek, SD. Decker was not afraid to point a finger at what he deemed responsible for the problem:

> The drive to earn money has taken control to such an extent that spiritual responsibilities are pushed to the side. The maxim 'the ends justify the means" has forced its way into our communities. Our children's education has become a low priority. In many communities, brothers are assigned to the school who are worthless everywhere else…In the [English] schools, we employ mostly unenlightened, worldly hirelings. This is a shocking shortcoming and sin which not even the Catholics of today practice [allusion to private Catholic schools]. This is a gross betrayal of our responsibility and is the fruit of our spiritual slothfulness and a lust for money. If things have deteriorated so far that our children are worth less than the pursuit of wealth, then we are long past all moderation.[44]

This, then, was the situation facing the Hutterite education system in 1930. For many of us looking back, it is difficult to understand why or how our ancestors could allow, in Victor Peters' words, this "outside agency that has penetrated Hutterian society most powerfully." There is a clear sense of inherent violence in Peters' use of the word penetrate that we should not miss. For centuries, our ancestors were willing to sacrifice their livelihoods and communities rather than allow their children to be taken out of their care. What stands between our children and the ever-increasing drive of acculturation and assimilation which began in the early 1900s and has become an acceptable part of our children's upbringing today? As we wrestle with what shape Hutterite education should take

---

44 John [Hans] J. Decker, "Overview of Hutterite History." Lecture, Hutterite Annual German School Conference. April 9, 1985, in author's collection.

Ekfrid School on Blumengart Community. Photo by G. G. Neufeld, no date.
[SOURCE: School Inspectors' Photographs, GR8461, A0233, C131-3. Archives of Manitoba.]

today, we would do well to reflect on what has changed during the past 100 years, and whether those changes are serving us well, and whether they are consistent with our identity as a faith community.

Reclaiming the Vision:
The Bruderhof and Hutterite Relationship

Our final topic in this lecture deals with the Hutterite relationship with the Bruderhof. This relationship began in the late 1920s and extends to the present. However, in this first lecture, we will only explore the history up to 1930. Subsequent lectures will continue the story.

To help us better understand the relationship between the Hutterites and the Bruderhof, I think it would be helpful to understand the historical context out of which both groups emerged. The Hutterites emerged out of the tremendous religious, political, intellectual, and cultural upheaval that we today know as the Protestant Reformation of the 16th-century. During the Reformation, much of Western culture was transformed as new ideas about religion, reason, and economics were developed. Some historians go so far as to suggest that capitalism itself was born or came into its own during this period. The rise of the Hutterite way of life can be interpreted, in part, as a protest against the ideas and practises of the emerging capitalist order. As the feudal system began to collapse, the balance of power began to shift, leading to social and cultural upheaval. The early Hutterites felt called to separate themselves from what they perceived as unjust systems of governance, be it religious or secular. In response to the practises of feudalism, they said "No!" to the inequality they saw around them. They said "No!" to the new system of capitalism, which was based on the principle of survival of the fittest. Instead, they developed a society which said "Yes!" to cooperation and communitarian socialism.

Similarly, some 400 years later, in the early 1920s, European society was once again undergoing profound convulsions and transformations. Following the destruction caused by World War I, Germany was thrown into economic and social disorder. The Treaty of Versailles, which was signed on June 28, 1918, forced Germany to take full responsibility for WWI and to pay exorbitant reparations to the Allies. Germany was unable to fulfil these unreasonable requests, and as a result, the government collapsed. In the long run, this collapse, the establishment of the new Weimar Constitution, and the Great Depression paved the way for Hitler's Nazi party to come to power in 1933.

The Bruderhof was born out of an intense search for a new way to construct human society following WWI. A protest movement known as the German Youth Movement further contributed to its identity:

> The years that followed [the war] brought widespread social change to Germany. In much the same way as American hippies rebelled against the complacent affluence of their parents during the Vietnam War, young people in the Weimar Republic turned their backs on the social conservatism and aristocratic pretensions of the failed Prussian empire.
> Thousands of them left the cities for the country, roaming farms and mountains in their search for truth and meaning in life. They lacked no divers-

> ity in background and opinion but held in common the belief that old structures and conventions must die and finally give way to something new. And although many of them soon drifted into the hedonism and moral decay that characterized the post-war period, others, like [Eberhard Arnold], saw in the Youth Movement an affirmation of their spiritual quest for wholeness.
>
> The Youth Movement sought answers to life's questions in the simplicity of rural life, in the trees and mountains and meadows, and in the poetry and literature of the romantics. They rejected the crass materialism of the cities in favor of the rural life, with its simple pleasures of folk-dancing and hiking, and turned their backs on the sterility of factory life to embrace the hard work—and the stench—of the farm.[45]

The devastating experience of the war psychosis which gripped Germany and the blatant inequalities between the rich and poor led Eberhard Arnold and a small group to seek after a different way of life—the way of Jesus and the Sermon on the Mount.[46]

Without going into further details, we can see that the Bruderhof and Hutterite movements both emerged in response to the massive social upheavals of their time and thus had much in common. Our focus will be on how the Bruderhof story connects to the Hutterite account. The book, *Brothers Unite*, provides the following introduction:

> [The Bruderhof story began in 1920 when] Eberhard and Emmy Arnold with their family and a few friends moved from Berlin to the little village of Sannerz in the Province of Hesse, Germany. They were earnestly seeking the will of God for their lives

---

45 Eberhard Arnold, *Eberhard Arnold: Writings Selected with an Introduction by Johann Christoph Arnold*, Modern Spiritual Masters Series (Maryknoll: Orbis Books, 2000), 17–18.
46 Ibid.

and had turned their backs on the unjust life of the world.
Through much sacrifice and trial and by the grace of God, a life of Christian church community came into being....
Eberhard Arnold believed that love and unity were the fruits of a Christian life. Therefore, he sought for brothers with whom he and his little group could unite. Through his studies in Anabaptist history, he discovered the beautiful writings of the Hutterian Brethren. Then he was made aware of the Hutterite Brothers still living in Bruderhofs in North America.[47]

By 1928, Arnold was corresponding with *Ältester* Elias Walter of the Dariusleut community, Stand Off, in Alberta, and openly discussing the possibility of his fledgling community in Germany joining the Hutterian Brethren. In 1929, he drafted a letter which he sent to all "Bruderhofs belonging to the church of God established by Jakob Hutter during the years 1533–1536."[48] In his letter, he formally requested that the Rhön Bruderhof be incorporated into the Hutterite church.

On the 18th of June, 1930, Arnold landed in Chicago and began a year of travel in which he would ultimately visit all 29 Hutterite communities in North America. From South Dakota, he made his way to Manitoba where the Schmiedeleut warmly received him. For his part, Arnold was deeply impressed by some of the leading Schmiedeleut ministers, including Peter Hofer, Joseph Kleinsasser (Sr. and Jr.), and Johann Hofer. At a meeting in Rosedale on September 14, 1930, Eberhard was carefully questioned as to why he and his community wanted to join the Hutterite church. At this meeting, the Schmiedeleut ministers discussed whether there was any precedent which could be helpful in this case, suggesting that they had forgotten how to do mission. The examples of Daniel Zwicker, Lorenz Huef, and Farwendel were examined. In particular, Farwendel's fervent entreaty and his acceptance while in pris-

---
47 *Brothers Unite*, VII.
48 Ibid.

Eberhard and Emmy Arnold. [SOURCE: http://www.eberhardarnold.com.]

on made a deep impression on all present.[49] Those present at the meetings felt it would be wrong to refuse Eberhard's request. On behalf of the Schmiedeleut Conference, *Ältester* Joseph Kleinsasser provided Eberhard Arnold with a letter of endorsement which he was to deliver to the Alberta Hutterite communities. In his letter, Joseph Kleinsasser wrote,

> We see no obstacle to the union [Eberhard] seeks with us, the Hutterian Brethren in general. For this reason, we gladly grant him our consent and agreement to this union and wish that the merciful God and heavenly Father will bless it in his love and unutterable grace. Indeed, may he himself lead and guide it all according to his will and pleasure, to the glory of his name and for the good of his people.[50]

Wherever Eberhard went, the Hutterites were impressed by his humility and zeal for communal life. After meeting with various leaders of the Alberta Hutterite conferences, Eberhard Arnold's request to join the Hutterite Church was granted. On the 9th of December, 1930, Eberhard was incorporated into the Hutterite church at

---

49 *The Chronicle of the Hutterian Brethren,* Volume I (Rifton: Plough Publishing House, 1987), 388–391.
50 *Brothers Unite,* 135.

Stand Off. Ten days later, he was confirmed in the Service of the Word:

> With this, Eberhard Arnold is given the task by the Church for Germany, to proclaim the Word of God there, to gather the zealous, and to establish the Bruderhof near Neuhof (Fulda) in Hessen-Nassau in the best order.[51]

With this act, the Bruderhof became the first Hutterite community to be simultaneously affiliated with the Dariusleut, Schmiedeleut, and Lehrerleut.[52] In addition to being given the responsibility for the church in Germany, Eberhard returned home with the prom-

---

51   Ibid., 185.
52   Ibid., 187.

Ältester **Elias Walter (1862–1938), Stand Off Community, AB. An exceptional leader and scholar.** [SOURCE: Author's collection.]

Eberhard Arnold, centre with tall hat, arriving at Maxwell in Manitoba, 1933.
[SOURCE: Jacob Kleinsasser Photo Collection.]

ise that the Hutterite church would send ministers to Germany to assist the fledgling group. This commitment, which at the time seemed inconsequential, would play a pivotal role in developing the relationship between the Schmiedeleut and the Bruderhof communities over the next 60 years.

During his year among the Hutterites, Arnold saw both the strengths and the weaknesses of the Hutterite way of life. Four hundred years of continuity had gifted the Hutterites with a rich and stable legacy which remains unrivalled among communal groups. At the same time, Eberhard saw how the Hutterites were slowly acculturating into the mainstream American and Canadian societies. Yes, their rural communities served somewhat as a buffer against the influences of 'the world,' yet Eberhard recognized that the proverbial Ark had begun to take on water. According to Eberhard, the Hutterite church was at its strongest during the first 170 years. One reason for this strength was that

> during this time it was never in doubt that the individual *Hof*, the individual *Haushabe* (household) is not the church. Rather, the church is the whole, unanimous body of all witnesses, glorified especially through martyrdom, and members of Christ's

Eberhard Arnold as Hutterite minister, ca. 1935. [SOURCE: http://www.eberhardarnold.com.]

> organism living in community here and now. And that the body is the church of God solely through the guiding and determining power of the Holy Spirit.[53]

What concerned Eberhard was the strong force of individualism that was expressing itself, not only in the individual Hutterites he met, but much more in the different Hutterite communities he visited. At the head of each community stood an individual, the spiritual leader, who often had a strong personality and who subconsciously projected his personality, theology, or agenda onto his community. Over the last 100 years, the role of leadership and governance within the Schmiedeleut conference has changed significantly, and there are numerous examples of the tension that has often developed between individual ministers, community mem-

---

53 *Brothers Unite*, 185.

bers, and the church elders. The 30 years after Michael Waldner's (*Schmied-Michl*) death mark a clear shift away from an episcopal vision of the church in which a *Vorsteher* or *Ältester* leads the church, to a more congregational pattern in which the church is governed by the congregations. However, if we look at the most recent conflicts in our conference, we can see that this issue is far from settled.

The Hutterite Vision

A final aspect of Eberhard Arnold's visit I wish to consider is the challenging questions he raised about what it means to be a Hutterite in the 21st-century. Eberhard and Hutterite elders like Elias Walter and Joseph Kleinsasser were struggling with the essential questions regarding the 'Hutterite vision.' When I am referring to the 'Hutterite vision,' I am alluding, perhaps presumptuously, to the 'Anabaptist vision' formulated in 1944 by Harold S. Bender, an influential Mennonite scholar who redefined the meaning of Anabaptism for many Mennonites. First, Bender identified discipleship, i.e., following Jesus in life and under the cross, as the essence of Anabaptism. Second, the 'Anabaptist vision' emphasized a church with voluntary membership, separation from the world, acceptance of persecution, and the exercise of brotherhood and sisterhood in economic affairs (mutual aid). Third, love and nonresistance applied to all human relationships.

Interestingly, fourteen years before Bender's formulation of the Anabaptist vision, Eberhard and the Hutterite leaders were discussing the nature of the 'Hutterite vision,' and what this means in its substance and vitality.[54] One of the most critical aspects of the vision includes a radical *Nachfolge Jesu* (discipleship), realized within the Gemeinde Christi (the gathered church of the faithful), which is modelled by the Gospel of Peace. The question they struggled with was how to reclaim the vision in the 20th-century. Some of the issues they discussed were:

1. The question of witness and mission. Since arriving in North America, the Hutterites growth had occurred by mean of natural expansion. Could more be done, especial-

---

[54] See also, Jerald Hiebert, *The Hutterite Story of a Pure Church*. Hiebert deals with the development of the Hutterite vision, or, more specifically, Christian Waldner's conception of what it means to be a Hutterite.

ly in light of the mission spirit during the first decades of Hutterite history?

2. The question of unity. In 1874, when the Hutterites were living in South Dakota, attempts were made to unify the three groups of Hutterites under one leader. Now they discussed whether there should again be one *Vorsteher* (*Ältester* over all the conferences), or at least a regular coming together of the leaders of each of the *Leut*?

3. The question of equality. Why were there rich and poor Hutterite communities? In particular, Eberhard was concerned over the practise of giving *Zehrgeld* [personal allowance] which he saw as leading to private property.[55]

These questions and issues are still relevant today. One of the reasons we celebrate anniversaries is to evaluate our progress on essential issues and to reflect on our identity. What answers can we give today to the questions about mission, unity, and equality? Are these questions even on our radar? Are we ready to reclaim the vision?

Without a doubt, the Hutterite/Bruderhof relationship is one of the most profound events in contemporary Hutterite historiography. Historian Leonard Gross compared this with similarly pivotal events in Hutterite history:

> Just as the Hutterian movement was regularly strengthened with the influx of Catholic Tiroleans (ca 1530), then of [crypto-]Lutheran Carinthians (1760s), and in Russia, of Mennonites (1800s), so in 1930, a new, yet well-established German-based Bruderhof also added its own richness and strength to the larger, ongoing movement called Hutterian.

> With each addition, there were changes in Hutterite culture. The sixteenth century saw mission and outreach, persecution notwithstanding; the seventeenth century saw a pulling back, caused by the ravages of warfare and pestilence. The eighteenth century yielded its own form of outreach, where

---

55   *Brothers Unite*, XVII–XVIII.

spirit and faith of Lutherans meshed with one specific history—that of the Hutterites. The nineteenth century brought in some Mennonites—and contacts, that perhaps changed the Hutterian structures, making each colony a bit more autonomous than had been the case in earlier Hutterian history. The twentieth century brought a group of Germans—but also, others from many lands, a sort of transcultural group—into the Hutterian fold, again, thanks to a historical awareness, leading to the discovery of the Hutterites. Here, indeed, is a twentieth century parallel to the eighteenth century Carinthian [crypto-]Lutherans.[56]

I wish to conclude this first lecture with a brief reflection on the significance of this centennial lecture, while at the same time offering a gentle criticism. The next three years (2018–2020) mark an important milestone in Hutterite history, namely, one hundred years of permanent settlement in Canada—one hundred years of successes, hardships, triumphs, and failures. Through great adversity, we have survived. We are here. Hutterites represent the largest communal society in the world today. Our current population is close to 50,000, and we have established more than 500 communities in Canada and the United States. For the most part, Hutterites have found a stable economic existence within the vast mosaic that is Canada. We are here, but are we flourishing? In many ways, we have primarily maintained—but not improved—our foreparents' vision for communal life.

The Hutterite way of life has faced numerous legal challenges over the last century and has held its own. Advancement in education, economics, farming, and industry have begun to reshape our communities in ways many Hutterites are not even aware of, and which we have to begin addressing with intention and care. Many of these changes are a mixed bag of blessings and burdens. There are, however, two areas in which we have changed very little: theological and historical thinking. With 'fear and trembling,' we have perpetuated what our foreparents established instead of building on what

---

56   Ibid., XVI.

they began. Both our spiritual teachings and our history books are evidence of our ancestors' exceptional education and vision. Great Hutterite scribes penned chronicles and theological writings which still astound scholars today. What have we contributed to this legacy? Have we turned our teachings, our history books, and our way of life into gods which we worship instead of the God they give witness to? So today, as we commemorate our centennial, we also ought to lament the fact that we have to a large extent failed to take up and pass on the pens of the great scribes, Caspar Braitmichel, Hauprecht Zappf, and Johannes Waldner. Thus, we have failed to continue the rich tradition of recording and reflecting on the history and theology of our people.

This failure has substantial implications for our present as well as our future. If we fail to teach our children where we have come from, we are in grave danger of failing to help them see where it is that we want them to go. In the same way, because we have not added in any significant way to our *Leadn* [church teachings] in order to address contemporary issues and questions, we are in danger of losing sight of our theology in the shifting sand of fundamentalism and other contemporary faith movements which are 'fundamentally' changing Hutterite communities in all conferences. Is this not a time of which the prophet Amos spoke when he said,

> The time is surely coming...when I will send a famine on the land; not a famine of bread, or a thirst for water, but of hearing the words of the Lord (8.11)?

Are our children 'hearing' our history and our theology, or are they living in a desert of our own creation? This is a dire reflection, but one that I hope leads us not to despair, but to action. We have to take our calling and our history seriously! Our future as a particular people of God depends on it![57] It is my fervent prayer that this lecture series and other historical projects, as well as advances in

---

57 See Deuteronomy 4.9: "Only take care, and keep your soul diligently, lest you forget the things that your eyes have seen, and lest they depart from your heart all the days of your life. Make them known to your children and your children's children." See also Deuteronomy 6.7: "You shall teach them diligently to your children, and shall talk of them when you sit in your house, and when you walk by the way, and when you lie down, and when you rise."

education, may serve as a vehicle by which we can begin a new re-formation and re-discovery of our faith and calling, and that some of the young men and women sitting here today may develop into our future historians and theologians.

In the next lecture, we will continue our narrative through the years 1930–1974. In that lecture, we will focus on the impact of the Great Depression, the Bruderhof departure from Germany, WWII, further land discrimination in Canada, interest in communal living from various seekers and converts, and the establishment of the 1950 Constitution of the Hutterian Brethren Church. The second lecture will conclude with the 1974 reuniting of the Bruderhof and the Hutterites.

LECTURE TWO
"Like the World, Only Later in Time"[1]

In our previous lecture, we learned how the Hutterites left the USA at the end of 1918 and resettled to Canada. For the most part, this migration took place over three to four years. However, in some cases, the move took considerably longer. For instance, Rockport (Lehrerleut) only sold its community in 1934. Even though families from Bon Homme, SD, immigrated to Canada to establish Bon Homme, MB, other families stayed behind. By 1934, these families bought the former Rockport, SD, site and built a new community. The Dariusleut community of Wolf Creek was only abandoned in 1930. By the 1930s, the majority of Hutterites had begun putting down permanent roots in Canada.

The Great Depression

On October 29, 1929, the value of the New York stock market plummeted, triggering the event we know today as the Great Depression. This was a time when Canadians suffered unprecedented levels of poverty due to unemployment. The extent of human misery resulting from the Great Depression and the creative responses it prompted in individuals are vividly described in letters written by Canadians recounting how families bartered food in exchange for medical services. Indeed, the Great Depression played a significant role in shaping Canadian social and political practises, particularly around health care. At the same time, the combination of the drought and the depression during the 1930s drove many

---

1   Marcus Bach, *Faith and my Friends* (Indianapolis: The Bobbs-Merrill Company, 1951), 141.

farmers from their land and this, in turn, contributed to a significant change in rural life, particularly within the Prairie Provinces. This phenomenon became known as urbanization and is an ongoing process. In the 1930s, the situation in the prairie regions was dire. Farmers who wished to leave their homes found it increasingly difficult to sell their farms. Merchants lacked cash customers. Municipalities went bankrupt as taxes remained unpaid.

Hutterite communities were better able to weather this storm than most. Victor Peters reports that while thousands of Canadians were destitute and depended on relief, Hutterites, with their self-sufficient economy, did not feel the economic depression as severely as the rest of Western Canada. Hutterites were not 'rich in money' but they were solvent enough to buy more land, support their local businesses, and pay their taxes. Municipalities considered Hutterite communities as assets.

So, up until the end of the Depression, the Hutterites were seen as a huge benefit to the Prairie Provinces. That all changed in 1939 when Canada declared war on Germany, and the Hutterites declared their unwillingness to participate in any way in the war effort. It was their pacifist convictions more than any other factor which turned public opinion against the Hutterites and led to some of the discriminatory regulations which we will explore in this lecture.

Despite Victor Peters' somewhat idyllic picture of Hutterite life during the Depression years, the Great Depression was still the Great Depression. The Hutterites might have weathered it better than many other Canadians, but the on-going drought and the economic downturn played a significant role in reshaping not only Canadian communities but also Hutterite communities. As we work our way through this lecture, it is crucial that we keep in mind this economic and political context.

By the 1930s, the consequences of the migration to Canada were becoming clear. Manitoba was not South Dakota. The harsh Manitoba winter and spring flooding must have been overwhelming. During this time of building up, very few Hutterites had the time to pick up a pen and write down their experiences. The drought, the depression, and the huge debt carried by the Schmiedeleut were a heavy burden. In some of the scant writings of this period, there is a clear sense of loss, hardship, even a longing to return to South Dakota, i.e. the 'fleshpots of Egypt.' This is most vividly captured in a song titled *Verloren in Kanada* [*Lost in Canada*], written or copied by Kathrina J. Waldner from Rosedale Community in Manitoba:

> …We came from the United States
> where everything had turned out well.
> Where will this end; who can make sense of it?
> Lost in Canada!
>
> Lost in Canada,
> in friendly Manitoba;
> yes, we owe half a million dollars.
> Isn't that over the top?
>
> That's how far we have fallen—
> isn't it lamentable?
> The old depart, leaving behind this place
> for the young to pay off….[2]

The refrain, "lost in Canada," poignantly captures the situation facing the Hutterites in Manitoba at this time. In 1918, when the Hutterite communities decided to flee to Canada, they could not have foreseen the economic and social difficulties they would have to face. Indeed, if they had, it is highly unlikely they would ever have left South Dakota. However, it might well be true that these shared hardships bound the Schmiedeleut communities closer together. The joint debts or loan not only forced the Schmiedeleut communities to work together, but it also reshaped their legal structure.

For instance, in 1931, the ten Schmiedeleut communities in Manitoba took steps to incorporate themselves to gain the legal status that would entitle them to borrow money. Their legal counsel, Er-

---

[2] This song was discovered among the papers of Paul Waldner (Rosedale, MB) and transcribed by Tony Waldner, Forest River Community, North Dakota. Transcription in author's collection, translated.

> **An Act to Incorporate the Barickman Hutterian Mutual Corporation.**
>
> [Assented to April 20th, 1931]
>
> **Preamble** WHEREAS a religious community of farmers exists in this province under the name of Barickman Colony of Hutterian Brethren, who have associated themselves together for the purpose of promoting and engaging in the Christian religion, Christian worship and religious education and teachings according to their religious belief, and of having, holding, using, possessing and enjoying all things in common, and who are desirous that the said religious community may be incorporated;

Articles of Incorporation for Bar[r]ickman, MB.
[SOURCE: *Statues of Manitoba 1931*, Volumes I & II. (Winnipeg: Philip Purcell, 1931), 528.]

nest Fletcher, caused several private members' bills to be passed in the Manitoba legislature which incorporated the communities as mutual corporations. This was a clear shift away from the more 'communal' structure practised by the Schmiedeleut in South Dakota during the days of the "Hutterische Brüder Gemeinde Corporation," as well as the spirit of 'joint' purchases and 'shared' responsibilities practised during the 1918 resettlement in Manitoba. As we saw in the previous lecture, the incorporation process was initially triggered by the lawsuit brought against the communities by the Great-West Life Insurance Company. The consequence of this shift was that the individual communities now operated much more independently of each other. This, in turn, eventually led to conflicts developing between the leaders who began to work more for the well-being of their communities than the well-being of the church as a whole.

The 1934 *Ältester* Election

Ever since the passing of Michael Waldner (*Schmied-Michl*) in 1889, the Schmiedeleut, unlike the other two *Leut*, had been without a *Vorsteher* or *Ältester*. Whenever issues arose, the minister who had been in the service the longest was asked to officiate. However, by 1933, this model was breaking down. The senior ministers of that era—Joseph Kleinsasser, Sr. (Milltown), David Hofer (James Valley), David Decker, Sr. (Barrickman), and Michael Waldner (Bon Homme, SD)—began a discussion about returning to the model of eldership practised by the early Hutterite church. In a letter dated November 17, 1933, David Decker, Sr. touched upon the core problem. He wrote:

> For the way we are handling things now is not good, for when serious issues or situations arise between different communities, somebody should be delegated to officiate. However, all ordained ministers are, so to speak, equal, with the exception that some have been in the service longer than others. Up until now, we have asked the one who has been in the service the longest to officiate. What gives this person more authority or freedom to act as an arbitrator in other communities' problems? And if he does, it gives the appearance that he has appointed himself to take care of something to which he has no more right or freedom than another confirmed servant. It does not befit us to take on something of our own accord. And that is why it is more correct that we assign somebody to know, guide, or promote important or difficult quarrels.[3]

By February 11, 1934, the four senior Schmiedeleut leaders had ironed out the procedure for how the Schmiedeleut would elect a new *Ältester*. This process was decidedly different from the process used by the Lehrerleut and Dariusleut today,[4] yet shared many similarities. One can see the main features of today's processes embedded within the various accounts recorded in the Hutterite Chronicles. In regards to the Schmiedeleut process, somebody—most likely the four senior Schmiedeleut ministers—must have read the various eldership accounts and crystallized the present-day process from those descriptions.

---

3   Joseph Kleinsasser to David Decker, Jr., 17 Nov. 1933, in author's collection.
4   When the Lehrerleut elect an *Ältester*, only ministers vote for the new *Ältester*. Potential candidates are nominated by the senior ministers with an age cap in place. The Dariusleut call a meeting of all the ministers where the senior ministers hold a closed meeting to choose an *Ältester*. The rest of the ministers are then summoned and informed as to the senior ministers' choice. A show of hands is required to indicate that a majority of the ministers are in agreement with the appointed *Ältester*.

It is important for us to think about how various tensions within the Hutterite congregations influenced the decision to return to leadership by an *Ältester*. For instance, the Schmiedeleut chose to incorporate each community as an individual unit made good sense economically, but came at the expense of the overall unity of the church. As the Schmiedeleut communities became more individualistic, it may well have had a similar effect on the different leaders. An *Ältester*, elected by all the voting members and authorized to his position by all the ministers, would be able to act as a mediator when difficulties arose within or between different communities or leaders.

When the final vote was tabulated in 1934, Joseph Kleinsasser from Milltown was, to use the expression commonly used by Hutterite chroniclers, 'given the responsibility of the church.' Thus, 45 years after the passing of Michael Waldner (*Schmied-Michl*), the Schmiedeleut once again elected an *Ältester* to lead the conference.

Visiting the Bruderhof:
David Hofer and Michael Waldner

By 1936, the Schmiedeleut communities in Manitoba were well enough established that they could begin to deal with other concerns. One pressing matter was the promise made to Eberhard Arnold in 1930 that the Hutterite Church in North America would send ministers to Germany to help instruct and assist the new Bruderhof congregation. On the 9th of December, a meeting was convened at the Rosedale Community in Manitoba where the matter was discussed. *Ältester* Joseph Kleinsasser suggested that one representative from each of the three *Leut* should be sent. However, when he addressed the issue with his Darius- and Lehrerleut counterparts, they declined to send a representative from their group. This made it necessary for the Schmiedeleut to select two brothers for the journey. David Hofer from James Valley, MB and Michael Waldner from Bon Homme, SD, were chosen.

The two Hutterite ministers arrived in England in February of 1937. While in England, they spent two months dealing with internal spiritual and economic questions and concerns at the Cotswold Bruderhof. On the 8th of April, they received an urgent phone call

Michael Waldner and David Hofer in Europe, 1937.
[SOURCE: *Treasures of Time* Collection, HBBC Digital Collection.]

asking them to come to the Rhön Bruderhof in Germany as soon as possible. They travelled through Holland and eventually arrived at the Rhön on the 9th of April.

A lot was going on in Germany in 1937. War clouds were gathering across much of Europe and Asia. Germany was secretly manufacturing and stockpiling weapons in preparation for an all-out war. Already in 1936, Germany had entered into what is known as the Anti-Comintern Pact with Japan. On November 6, 1937, Italy and Spain also joined the agreement, thereby forming the group that would later be known as the Axis Powers. Britain and France, as well as other nations, were also forming secret alliances. All of Europe was a powder keg primed and ready to explode. As the powerful nations of the world prepared for war, the two Hutterite ministers, for the most part utterly oblivious to the great menace mounting around them, quietly crossed the border into Germany.

If the two Hutterite ministers were oblivious to what was going on in Germany, the brothers and sisters at the Rhön Bruderhof were not. Since 1933, this small community had lived under the constant threat of the Nazis. The Bruderhof children and young men of military age had all been quietly sent out of the country to the independent principality of Lichtenstein. Once compulsory military conscription was introduced in Germany, the young men escaped to the Cotswold Bruderhof in England (established in 1936). When the two brothers arrived, they were soon informed about the dire situation. Fearlessly, they called upon the local *Landrat* [district official] who had made it quite clear that the Rhön Bruderhof was no longer wanted in the area. The two Hutterite brothers paid him a friendly visit to try softening him up. The Bruderhof members introduced the brothers as "two representatives of Germans living abroad, from America, elders of the *Gemeinde* over there [America]."

From this discussion, the brothers all realized that the Rhön Bruderhof was doomed. They had to sell everything as soon as possible and leave. In a letter written to *Ältester* Joseph Kleinsasser, David Hofer describes what happened next:

> On the 14th of April, Michael Waldner and I were in Eberhard Arnold's room when Hans Meier came in and told us to prepare ourselves as he had seen a large number of police coming down the hill towards the community. He said, 'They cannot do anything to you.' I walked out of our room and went outside. The yard was already full of police. They had sabers and revolvers in hand, all equipped to strangle and stab. One of them yelled at me,

'Where is Hans Meier?' I replied, 'Doubtless in the house.'

'Call him out here,' was the next order. When I came back with Hans Meier, the man greeted him with a '*Heil Hitler.*' Hans Meier merely answered with a 'Good day.' After this, the chief officer read out an order which stated, 'I inform you that the Rhön Bruderhof is now dissolved by the state and must exist no longer. From now on it is to be called 'Sparhof' and as you are the leader of this Bruderhof, I demand all books and keys from you. I inform you also that within twenty-four hours, all must leave the place.'[5]

David Hofer's diary gives a graphic account of how the police systematically searched the *Hof* and took whatever they wanted. On several occasions, David Hofer fearlessly approached the commanding officer and objected. Later, when David Hofer realized that the Nazi officers intended to scatter the members in all directions, he once again approached the officers:

> I told them that what we had experienced here today was entirely uncalled for and that we had not expected such a thing of Germany…I told them that they were worse than the Americans. Then they at once asked me, 'How?' I told them that when we as Germans were called up in the last war to do military service against Germany, we objected and refused to do it, as these, our brothers, had just done. Then we asked our government in the USA to let us have the freedom to leave the country.… we asked to sell all we had and leave nothing behind us—all of which was not refused us by the American government.[6]

It is unclear what would have happened to the brothers and sisters at the Rhön Bruderhof had David Hofer and Michael Hofer

---

5   David Hofer and Michel Waldner to Joseph Kleinsasser, 2 May 1937, in author's collection.
6   Ibid.

not been present. What is clear is that David Hofer's courage and negotiation skills on behalf of the Bruderhof members changed whatever outcome the Nazis might have intended. Suffice it to say that the brothers and sisters of the Rhön Bruderhof were eventually allowed to leave Germany and travel first to Lichtenstein and then onward to England. Arnold Snyder, one of our most prominent Anabaptist historians, once stated that to be an Anabaptist was to make "a faith decision that directly confronted and challenged the social, religious, and political status quo."[7] This is precisely what the Bruderhof members did and consequently, like so many others in history, paid a steep price.

1939–1944: World War II and Alternative Service

Back in Manitoba, war clouds were also darkening the prairie skies. The Great Depression had come to an end. Less than two years after David Hofer and Michael Waldner returned from their journey, all of Europe was once again at war. On September 9, 1939, Canada formally declared war against Germany. However, many Canadians opposed the Canadian government's decision. French Canadians, for example, felt the war was a European affair and that Canada had no obligation to get involved. Others opposed the war on religious grounds. These people became known as 'conchies' or conscientious objectors.

The Mennonite and Hutterite leaders were deeply concerned about whether the Canadian government would introduce conscription. The initial response they received from Prime Minister Mackenzie King's office was that there would be no conscription. However, in 1940, Canada suddenly implemented the National Resources Mobilization Act, which required enlistment for home defence. Under this act, everyone between the ages of 18 and 36 had to register with the military.

Why the sudden change? The war in Europe had just taken a drastic turn. In the spring of 1940, German forces invaded and defeated France, Holland, and Belgium. Suddenly, Canada was Great Britain's most important ally in the war. Much to the relief of many of

---

[7] C. Arnold Snyder, *Anabaptist History and Theology: An Introduction* (Kitchener: Pandora Press, 1995), 2.

Certification of Medical Examination for Jacob Kleins[as]ser, 1943.
[SOURCE: Jacob Kleinsasser Collection.]

the peace churches in Canada, by this time provisions were already in place for alternative service or work under the oversight of the National War Services Board. Hutterites, like all COs, could apply for a postponement of military service. These initial postponements allowed the Hutterite COs to return home to their communities. However, by May of 1941, COs were being assigned to work in forestry, national parks, and road construction projects. The initial mobilization of the COs was slowed because there weren't enough camps for all the COs. The Hutterites, because they formed a relatively small percentage of Canada's COs, faced comparatively low pressure to participate.[8] However, by 1942, public displeasure began to be focused against the Hutterites whose young men got to stay at home while other Canadians were bleeding and dying in the war. The public demanded that Hutterites and other COs be forced to participate in the war effort.

---

8   Mennonites (4,425), Hutterites (482), Doukobors (406), Jehovah's Witnesses (172), total COs in Canada was 6,158. J. A. Toews, *Alternative Service in Canada during World War II* (Publication Committee of the Canadian Conference of the Mennonite Brethren Church, 1959), 99.

Initially, Hutterite young men reported to their local doctors for their medical examinations. Sympathetic doctors often granted them medical discharges. However, the government grew suspicious of this ploy and eventually ordered the Hutterite men to appear at the barracks in Winnipeg. Those young men who were found to be in excellent health soon received orders to report for alternative service duty. The Hutterite elders, for their part, felt that their communities and young men were being unfairly targeted. Manitoba's chief justice, John Adamson, acknowledged as much in a letter to *Ältester* Joseph Kleinsasser. Adamson wrote,

> I venture to say that there is no English-speaking community in all of Canada which has not got more boys away from their homes and families, frequently wives and children, than your community has in alternative service.[9]

Adamson was also quick to point out the fact that anything less would likely cause a huge backlash.

Adamson was right. By 1944, public sentiment had decidedly turned against the Hutterites. The chief complaint against them was that Hutterites were becoming rich while everyone else was busy fighting the war. This eventually led to the passage of the Land Sale Prohibitions Act in Alberta.

Alternative Service Camps

By the end of the war, there were roughly 29 Alternative Service Camps in Canada. These camps were located in Ontario, Manitoba, Saskatchewan, Alberta, and British Columbia. In Manitoba, some of the young men were assigned to help local farmers or were sent to work at Clear Lake, Manitoba.

Others were sent to work in the forestry camps in Saskatchewan or British Columbia. Their work consisted of clearing trees left standing by lumber companies or cutting down trees left behind after forest fires. Another task was planting trees.

By the end of the war, most of the Hutterite young men were being sent to work at the Port Arthur Grain Terminal in Thunder Bay,

---

9   J. E. Adamson to Joseph Kleinsasser 27 March 1943, in author's collection.

As COs, most Hutterite young men worked in the forestry industry. Others worked at Clear Lake, MB or the Port Arthur Grain Terminal in present-day Thunder Bay, ON. [SOURCE: Author's collection.]

where they unloaded grain cars. Two boys could unload eight train cars in one day. Others loaded the grain onto ships.

As the war continued to rage in Europe, Canada became England's primary food supplier. The drought had ended by 1939, and the Canadian prairies were producing an astonishing amount of wheat. Production was so high that it created a surplus which the Canadian government struggled to handle. England, however, desperately needed more protein and called upon its main ally to deliver. This triggered what some historians called the most profound transformation in the history of Canadian agriculture as the country's farmers changed direction and produced the required foodstuffs in such vast quantities that their contribution to the Allied victory was universally recognized. Canada's Prairie Provinces shifted from an economy geared primarily for grain farming to mixed farming. Government incentives encouraged farmers to diversify beyond wheat production to raise pork, beef, and poultry products. These changes would, in turn, have a profound impact on Hutterite agricultural practises for decades to come.

Economic Expansion and Discrimination

One of the main charges brought against the Hutterites during the war years was that they were taking advantage of the relatively cheap land prices to buy up large quantities of land which should

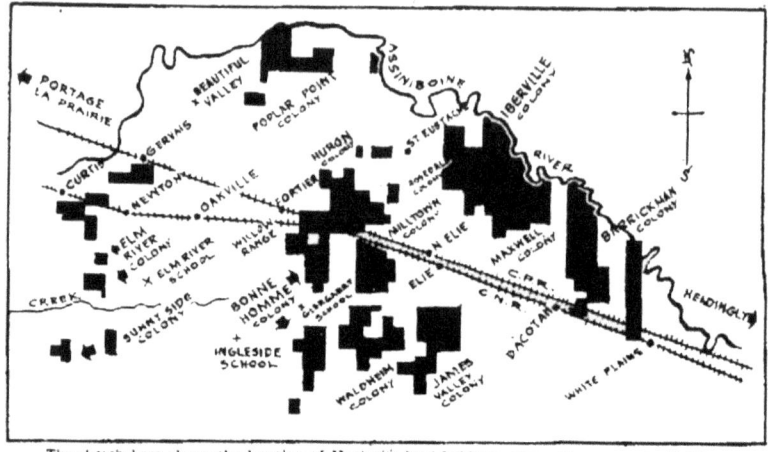

Hutterite land holdings along the Assiniboine River.
[SOURCE: *Winnipeg Free Press*, April 21, 1947.]

have been reserved for members of the Canadian armed forces. An increasingly hostile public, particularly in the province of Alberta, demanded that action be taken to limit the growth of Hutterite communities. This eventually led to the passage of the 1942 Land Sales Prohibition Act in Alberta which forbade the sale and lease of land to Hutterites. Initially, the prohibition was supposed to be in place until the end of the war, but it remained in effect until 1947. After 1947, the Alberta legislature passed the Communal Properties Act which allowed Hutterite communities to purchase land but it prohibited them from purchasing land within forty miles of an existing community and required that new communities not possess more than 6400 acres. The legislation also specified a 90-day waiting period during which land must be offered for public sale before any Hutterite community could buy it. This act was only repealed in 1973. This case is of historical interest because it tested the validity of what might be considered discriminatory legislation in Canada. The case also demonstrates how fickle the Supreme Court of Canada was in protecting the fundamental freedoms of Canadians.[10] Victor Peters observed:

---

10   M. M. Litman, "Communal Properties Act Case," *The Canadian Encyclopedia*, May 06, 2006. Accessed July 13, 2019. https://www.thecanadianencyclopedia.ca/en/article/communal-properties-act-case.

> The Communal Property Act, despite its severity, did not appease the agitators; indeed, the demand after 1956 was for the forcible dissolution of all Hutterian Communities. Meanwhile, the act and the agitation have affected not only the Hutterians but also farmers who would like to sell their land for the best price possible but are unable to do so because Hutterians are often not permitted to buy it.[11]

In Manitoba, a province older than Alberta and with a more established ethnic pattern, the anti-Hutterite agitation took a different form. At no time has there been a danger of violence. One important reason for this was the influence of the two daily Winnipeg papers, the *Free Press* and the *Tribune*. In their editorials both consistently counselled moderation on the Hutterian question.[12]

As Victor Peters pointed out, the Hutterite problem was handled differently in Manitoba than in Alberta, but the underlying prejudices were the same. The movement against the Hutterites in Manitoba initially gained momentum from meetings held in 1947 at Oakville and St. Eustache. Historically, these two towns were trading centres. However, much of their former business had shifted to the faster-growing town of Portage la Prairie. At the same time, the Prairie Provinces also experienced a sharp increase in urbanization which led to an alarming decline of the population in rural communities. There was also a shift away from the Prairie Provinces as a whole (a trend which has recently reversed).[13] These and other disruptions in the status quo of the region generated dissatisfaction. Somebody needed to be blamed for these economic changes and the Hutterites were a suitable scapegoat. Developments in the Manitoba legislature stimulated the impetus for the protest movement against the Hutterites. As we saw earlier, it had been the practise to incorporate new communities by an act of the legislature. However, in 1946 bills to incorporate new Hutterite

---

11 Victor Peters. *All Things Common*, 56.
12 Ibid.
13 From 2011 to 2014, the three Prairie Provinces (Alberta, Saskatchewan and Manitoba) had a higher population growth than the national average, and the highest population growth among the provinces. This was a first since 1971.

Dr. Marcus Bach (1906–1995). [SOURCE: http://www.truthunity.net/people/marcus-bach]

communities had been rejected by the Private Bills Committee. The committee members were no doubt sensitive to public opinion and the widespread popular support received by the Alberta restrictions.

Soon after the 1947 meetings, the legislature appointed a special committee to study the Hutterite problem and come up with some recommendations. Farmers and local merchants from the area between Headingley and Portage la Prairie submitted briefs to the committee in which they demanded restrictive legislation. However, the response of individuals and groups opposed to such legislation[14] was much stronger than it had been in Alberta. Among these supporters was Dr. Marcus Bach, an anthropologist from Iowa State University. John J. Maendel, the steward from the New Rosedale Community, was a friend of Marcus Bach and asked him to represent the Hutterites in the legislature. Marcus Bach came, but the message he gave the Manitoba legislators shocked his Hutterite listeners. He began his presentation by pointing out the fact that the Hutterites had the distinction of being the oldest communal group in the Western world. He then told the committee that the United States had seen over 128 failed communal groups.[15] All these groups thought they had developed the perfect system, but all disappeared. Bach advised,

> Do not legislate against the communes.... If the Hutterites are treated with understanding and respect, they will soon be assimilated.... This investigation is not concerned with land acts and slave clauses. It is interested in learning whether the Hutterites will ever become Canadianized. I think they will. But persecution and legislation won't hurry things. When groups are discriminated against, they become unfortunate minority problems. Tolerant practices bring groups into society and hasten the assimilative process....
> I love the Hutterites, and I respect their ideals, but I do not believe that they can hold back the world any longer. I say this even though I have walked the streets of Amana with a Hutterite and he said, 'This will never happen to us.' But it is happening. Why? For good or ill there is a spirit in the world which is so strong that no one can subjugate it. Some call it

---

14 Among those opposed were the Manitoba Civil Liberties Association, The Manitoba Conference of the United Church, Dr. E. M. Howse of Westminster Church in Winnipeg, and John A. McDowell, a member of the committee and legislative member for Iberville constituency.

15 In actual fact, the number was 281. See Clifford F. Thies. "The Success of American Communes," *Southern Economic Journal* 67, no. 1 (2000): 186–99.

The January 1988 cover illustration of the *Alberta Report*. [SOURCE: HBBC Digital Collection.]

the *Weltgeist*. Others call it the American way. But whatever it is, we know that no fence can keep it out, no wall can hold it back, no commune boundary can say, 'You shall not pass.'[16]

The committee members asked Dr. Bach for recommendations that would hasten assimilation. He gave them four:

---

16   Marcus Bach. *Faith and my Friends*, 138–139.

1. an improved school curriculum,
2. tolerance and understanding of the Hutterian religion,
3. participation by the Hutterites in provincial and national elections, and
4. rejection of the proposed land act.

John J. Maendel and other Hutterite leaders were disappointed by Dr. Bach's assessment. John stated,

> If you expect us to change our schools and if you think we should take part in national affairs, then, of course, you are only leading us closer to your expectation. I suppose one way of making prophecy come true is to predict a thing and then make it happen. But it will not happen this time. We are rooted and grounded in our faith, and on that faith, we stand.[17]

However, other Hutterites quietly agreed with Dr. Bach:

> 'The young people are different from the way they used to be. They do not work as we worked. They are more difficult to discipline. They do not see how precious our faith is and at what cost it was bought.'
>
> 'Sometimes,' said another, 'I think that we are today like the world was fifty years ago. Later we will be like the world was twenty-five years ago. Later still we will be like the world is today. We are like the world; only we are later in time.'[18]

In the end, the committee chose not to enact restrictive legislation; instead, it made several recommendations bearing on the curriculum for Hutterite schools and suggested amendments in the Colony Corporation Act which would ensure that anyone leaving a Hutterite community would receive an equitable share.

In 1948, the Manitoba legislature appointed a new committee to explore the possibility of passing legislation that would award an

---

17 Ibid, 141.
18 Ibid.

equal share to departing members. However, in the end, the committee recognized that the proposed bill contained a threat to the very existence of the Hutterite communities. The committee's original recommendation was moved and defeated on the floor of the Manitoba legislature.

For some years after 1948, the Hutterite question remained dormant, but it came up again at a convention of the Union of Manitoba Municipalities in 1954. A resolution was passed asking the government to restrict both the purchase of land by Hutterite communities and also their location. The chief objections to the Hutterites were that:

1. they contributed to the disorganization of existing communities,
2. they took no interest in the welfare of the broader community, its schools and social functions, and
3. they did not support local business.[19]

In 1957, fearing that the renewed agitation would lead to restrictive legislation, the Hutterites of Manitoba sought a compromise. With the provincial government acting as a mediator, the representatives of the Union of Manitoba Municipalities and Hutterite communities signed a 'Gentlemen's Agreement' in which the latter accepted virtually all of the municipalities' demands. They promised to limit the landholdings of new communities to 5,120 acres and to limit the number of communities per municipality to two unless the municipality itself was willing to accept more communities, and they agreed that new communities would not be closer than ten miles from each other. The Gentlemen's Agreement, which was in effect for twelve years, was unethical and discriminatory. The *Winnipeg Tribune* expressed as much in its editorial:

> It is to be sincerely hoped that the agreement will put an end to the essentially undemocratic demands which have surrounded the Hutterite question in Manitoba in recent years.[20]

---

19   Victor Peters, *All Things Common*, 59–60.
20   Editorial, "Voluntary Hutterite Curb," *Winnipeg Tribune*, April 29, 1957.

The Land Sales Prohibition Act and Gentlemen's Agreement were definite proof of the price people have to pay simply for being different. For many people, there is nothing more unsettling than people who look and act differently. Differences make some feel uncomfortable. "There ought to be a law or a wall that protects us from such people," these people say. These discriminatory acts and agreements were such attempts to 'wall in,' or to bring about, in Victor Peters' words, "the forcible dissolution of all Hutterite communities."[21] Doubtless, this discriminatory behaviour was fuelled by the deep-seated resentment that many Canadians felt because of the Hutterites' pacifist stance during the war, and the fact that they chose to isolate themselves from the rest of society.

Interestingly enough, a few months after the Gentlemen's Agreement was signed, the Rosedale Community negotiated for land in the Municipality of Elton, north of Brandon. Even though the proposed purchase met all the requirements of the Gentlemen's Agreement, the municipality asked the government to block the sale. The government ignored the appeal and allowed the purchase.[22]

By 1969, the Gentlemen's Agreement was no longer a workable solution. The Union of Manitoba Municipalities proposed that the two parties enter into a new agreement. The proposed agreement was essentially the same as the old agreement except that the amount of land a Hutterite community could own was increased to 9,600. To my knowledge, this agreement was never ratified by the Hutterite communities. The following year, New Rosedale Community purchased "land that was in clear violation of the agreement when the NDP government sold them the Macdonald Airport (a former Commonwealth Air Training base)."[23] In Premier Edward Schreyer's words, the Gentlemen's Agreement

> prohibiting such a purchase constituted discrimination against the Hutterites, and was no longer valid. The Manitoba Human Rights Commis-

---

21 Victor Peters, *All Things Common*, 56.
22 "Petition Asks Control of Hutterite Expansion," *Winnipeg Free Press*, August 16, 1957; "Government Refuses Bid to Curb Hutterites," *Winnipeg Free Press*, August 19, 1957.
23 Yossi Katz and John Lehr, *Inside the Ark*, New Edition (Regina: University of Regina Press, 2014), 154.

sion[24] supported this decision...and claimed that the agreement was in contravention of Canadian law regarding human rights. The Union gave up its threat to prosecute the Hutterites for violation of the agreement, and Airport Colony was established on the site.[25]

The restrictive legislation in Alberta and Manitoba contributed measurably to the strengthening of ties between the three *Leut*. Bertha Clark, a sociologist who spent a considerable time among the Hutterites in South Dakota, predicted as much when she wrote:

> Persecution from without, if it does not crush out life entirely, always strengthens the bond among those who have endured it in common, and this has been a great factor in Hutterian experience.[26]

Similarly, Canadian author C. Frank Steele observed, "Someday there may come disintegration from within; certainly, pressure from without the colonies will not bring it about."[27]

The 1951 Constitution

The law limiting Hutterites from leasing or purchasing land had the intended purpose of reducing the Hutterites' cohesiveness by keeping communities more isolated from each other. It had, however, the opposite effect. In August of 1950, the leaders of the various *Leut* or Conferences assembled to formulate a constitution for all Hutterites: the Constitution of the Hutterian Brethren Church.

---

24 The Canadian Bill of Rights was enacted by the Parliament of Canada on August 10, 1960 under the leadership of Prime Minister Diefenbaker, who had been campaigning for the protection of human rights since becoming a Member of Parliament in 1945. Concern for civil liberties had surfaced during this time partly in response to the atrocities and human suffering which occurred during World War II. Further impetus for human rights protection under domestic law came in 1948 with the adoption of the United Nations Universal Declaration of Human Rights which had a clear and significant influence on the Bill of Rights. Most provisions of the Bill of Rights have been replicated and enshrined in the Canadian Charter of Rights and Freedoms, 1982.
25 Yossi Katz and John Lehr, *Inside the Ark*, 154.
26 Bertha W. Clark, "The Huterian [*sic*] Communities, Part II" *Journal of Political Economy*, 32, No. 4 (August 1924): 484.
27 C. Frank Steele, "Canada's Hutterite Settlement," *Canadian Geographical Journal* 22 (June 1941): 314.

Constitution
of
Hutterian Brethren Church
and
Rules as to Community of Church Property

The title page of the 1951 Constitution of the Hutterian Brethren. [SOURCE: Author's collection.]

The purpose of the association was to enable the Hutterite Church to jointly lobby the federal government in Ottawa whenever discriminatory issues arose which challenged the community as a whole. The constitution specified that the Hutterite Church is divided into three *Leut*. The Board consisted of nine members—three from each *Leut*. This board was to meet biennially.[28] At the same time, a formal church structure was seen as a way to create a sense of shared unity and purpose within the greater Hutterite body. If the purpose of the restrictive laws was to reduce the cohesiveness within the Hutterite congregations, the 1951 Constitution could be seen as an attempt to counteract this adverse effect. As we will see in our last lecture, this only worked as long as there was "pressure from outside the colonies" but ultimately led to "disintegration from within" when pressures from outside ceased.[29]

The (Ongoing) Attack on Education

Today, there are approximately 462 Hutterite communities scattered across the USA and Canada. In Manitoba, there are about 107 Schmiedeleut communities. Nearly half of Schmiedeleut schools are staffed by Hutterite teachers and the rest are staffed by

---

28 The Federal Constitution should not be confused with the Articles of Association which govern the day-to-day function of individual Hutterite communities. The Articles of Association predate the Federal Constitution by at least 50 years. According to Zieglschmid, the original Articles of Association were drafted with the help of the Harmonist Society of Pennsylvania. See *Das Klein-Geschichtsbuch*, 462.

29 C. Frank Steele, "Canada's Hutterite Settlement," 314.

Many rural schools were closed during consolidation. Some of these schools were re-purposed by Hutterite communities either as dwellings or schools. Shown here is Mountain View School which became Parkview School, Riding Mountain, MB.
[SOURCE: http://www.mhs.mb.ca/docs/sites/mountainviewschool.shtml]

non-Hutterite teachers. If this same scenario had been played out in our foreparents' days, they would have undoubtedly viewed it as a regrettable development or, at the very least, a severe failure on their part. This is particularly true when we look at how public education has been used in the past to disrupt minority cultures and force them to assimilate into the host society.

In 1967, Victor Peters wrote,
> One of the ultimate objectives [of the public school] is to integrate or assimilate the Hutterians into the larger Canadian population stream. Its overt objective is to educate young Hutterians, but it also has a covert objective of influencing them to turn away from what are regarded by outsiders as outmoded ways and institutions. The public school as an agent of social disorganization, poses a sustained threat to Hutterian survival.[30]

Now compare this statement to statements made by two Canadian government officials regarding the government's stated purpose of education among the First Nations people in Canada. "Our object

---

30   Victor Peters, *All Things Common*, 137.

is to continue until there is not a single Indian [sic] in Canada that has not been absorbed into the body politic,"[31] and, "We must face realistically the fact that the only hope for the Canadian Indian [sic] is eventual assimilation into the white race."[32] If you are in any way familiar with the devastation brought about by the Canadian Residential School system and the Sixties Scoop, it is not hard to see the 'covert' educational agenda which a hostile public has periodically tried to force on the Hutterites. Such was the case in 1947 and 1954 when the Union of Manitoba Municipalities lobbied the government to make changes to the Hutterite educational system which would "assist in assimilating" Hutterites into the greater Canadian culture.[33]

In 1967, the Manitoba Government tried to force the Hutterites to send their children into consolidated schools which were, in some cases, no longer located on the Hutterite communities. E. A. Fletcher, the legal counsel for the Hutterites, presented a brief on behalf of the Hutterite Church in which he argued that forcing the Hutterite children into consolidated schools would be a form of discrimination which might cause serious mental injury:

> It has been the experience of the Hutterian Brethren in their entire history that this tension has never diminished, but will continue to increase so long as there are bigots, bullies and people who, in their zealous way, cannot suffer from having someone within their midst who is different, strange or peculiar to his way or belief, dress or manner of speech.[34]

The consolidated schools issue soon passed. However, some Hutterite elders were becoming increasingly concerned about the education of Hutterite children. One such leader was Jacob D. Maendel from Fairholme Community. In 1960, he encouraged his

31 The Truth and Reconciliation Commission of Canada, *Honouring the Truth, Reconciling for the Future: Summary of the Final Report of the Truth and Reconciliation Commission of Canada*, 2015, 3.
32 *Summary of the Final Report of the Truth and Reconciliation Commission*, 6.
33 Victor Peters, *All Things Common*, 58.
34 Fletcher and Baker ["Counsel for the Hutterian Brethren of Manitoba"] to "The Unitary School Division of Manitoba," 1967, in author's collection.

Peter Maendel (Fairholme, MB), April 1977.
[SOURCE: PC 18, A.81-12, Winnipeg Tribune Personalities Collection Winnipeg Tribune fonds, University of Manitoba Archives & Special Collections, Winnipeg, Manitoba, Canada.]

brother, Peter Maendel, to acquire the required certifications to become a teacher. Even though this move was widely criticized within the Hutterite world, it was Jacob's vision which began the process which saw certified Hutterite educators once more teaching Hutterite children. These were pioneering steps, and it took almost 30 years before any concerted effort would be made by the Hutterite communities to take back more control of their school system.

In the final section of this lecture, I will explore a number of important topics which round off the years 1930–1976.

Seekers and Converts: The Almost Great Awakening

One of the most unexpected by-products of all the discrimination experienced by the Hutterites was that it brought them into the public consciousness. For many decades, the Hutterites had been the "*stillen im Lande* [quiet in the land]," by keeping to themselves as much as possible. From the 1920s onward, however, Hutterites found themselves increasingly in the public spotlight. Even though many of the articles attacked the Hutterites, others painted an almost idyllic picture of community life. During the early 1960s, the hippie subculture began to develop across the United States, and the Hutterite practise of communal and rural living was appealing to a growing number of people, though we disappointed them in the areas of music and recreational drug use. Other people became interested in the Hutterite way because they were seeking a more authentic Christian life. All across North America, people of all walks of life were disillusioned by their church's outdated practises, struggles over social justice issues, and fear of the nuclear arms race. Something was "blowing in the wind." Although their legacy can't be fully explored in these lectures, some of the more prominent personalities who had a significant and lasting impact on Hutterites are Julius Kubassak,[35] Terrel Miller,[36] Ronald Dorn,[37] and the Baer family.[38]

The Bruderhof Communities

In our final topic, we pick up the Bruderhof story again. In the first lecture, we took the story up to 1937, when they were in the process of moving from Germany to England to escape the Nazis. How-

---

35 See Peter G. Clark, *The Brethren of Early Christianity: A Study of a World Rejecting Sect* (Master's Thesis, McMaster University, 1967); also Christina E. Moss, "'A Song for Brother Julius,' Revisited: On Growing Up On the Community Farm of the Brethren," *Anabaptist Historians*, August 14, 2018. Accessed July 16, 2019. https://anabaptisthistorians.org/2018/08/14/a-song-for-brother-julius-revisited-on-growing-up-on-the-community-farm-of-the-brethren/.

36 Rod A. Janzen, *Terry Miller: The Pacifist Politician: From Hutterite Colony to State Capitol* (Freeman: Pine Hill Press, 1986).

37 Mary-Ann Kirkby, *I am Hutterite: The Fascinating True Story of a Young Woman's Journey to Reclaim her Heritage* (Prince Albert: Polka Dot Press, 2007; Nashville: Thomas Nelson, 2011).

38 Mary Irwin Baer, ed., *Ehpraim & Lovina Baer Family History Book*, 6th edition. (Portage la Prairie: published by author, 2015).

ever, because of the war, the German-speaking Bruderhof members were not welcome in England. Several options were explored, including a possible move to Canada or the United States. However, again, due to the onset of the war, German-speaking pacifists were unwelcome. Eventually, the Bruderhof found a welcome haven in Paraguay. By 1941 the Cotswold Bruderhof in England was sold, and all but three members and seven seekers had relocated to Paraguay.[39] However, due to some unforeseen difficulties, the remaining brothers had to keep living on at Cotswold, even though it was already sold. People who had heard about the Bruderhof still came to visit. By Christmas of 1941, the little group in England had grown to twenty. As the war was now in full swing, it became impossible for these new members to leave England. Because Cotswold had been sold, the little group eventually had to go and find a new place to establish a community, and so Wheathill Bruderhof was born.

Fast forward to 1949: the Schmiedeleut in Manitoba called a meeting where they decided that two ministers, Samuel Kleinsasser from Sturgeon Creek and John Wipf from Spink Community, SD, would be sent to visit the Paraguay communities. The elders in Manitoba had heard rumours about disunity, disorder, and flagrant violation of church *Ordnungen*.

The Bruderhof situation in Asuncion, Paraguay demands a brief description. In Paraguay, the Bruderhof communities had established themselves in three communities: Ibate, Lomi Hobi, and Isla Margareta. Several years before the visit of the two Hutterite ministers, the Bruderhof communities went through an internal struggle. For instance, in 1942, a serious conflict developed among the Bruderhof leaders over the community's direction. Some, including Eberhard Arnold's wife, Emmy, argued that the original Bruderhof vision was rooted in a Pietistic faith in Jesus Christ, not primarily in communitarian ideals. Eventually, the church leadership, headed by the founder's son-in-law Hans Zumpe, banished the dissidents from the Bruderhof. The expelled members were eventually permitted to rejoin the community. One of them, Johann Heinrich [Heini] Arnold, a son of Eberhard and Emmy

---

39   Approximately 350 people.

Samuel Kleinsasser (1895–1960), Sturgeon Creek Community, MB.
[SOURCE: Jacob Kleinsasser Collection.]

Arnold, was sent with his family to New York to raise funds. By 1954, Heini Arnold played an important role in establishing the Woodcrest Bruderhof.[40]

When Samuel Kleinsasser and John Wipf visited the Bruderhof in 1950, these tensions were playing out in the background. Heini Arnold was already in New York, and a new chapter in the Bruderhof history was about to begin. Throughout their visit, the two brothers were disturbed by the disunity and disrespect they experienced. In particular, they attributed the disunity to the fact that the

---

40 Merrill Mow, *Torches Rekindled: The Bruderhof's Struggle for Renewal* (Rifton: Plough Publishing House, 1991), 13.

Bruderhof was not complying with the Hutterite *Ordnungen* on some fronts. Some of the critical points of concern from the Hutterites' perspective were smoking,[41] movies, musical instruments, unbaptized sisters not wearing head-coverings, lack of beards for married men, women participating in council,[42] the prayers before and after the meal not being the same as those in use among the Hutterite communities (both for adults and children). What became clear to both sides is that the two groups had very different visions of what church life should look like. During their visit, the two Hutterite ministers raised some concerns they felt were hindering a fuller uniting of the two groups. The Bruderhof countered with their own list of concerns and said, "We'll accept yours, if you accept ours." Later, the Bruderhof leaders appealed for tolerance:

> There may well be certain issues in which we have differing practices, yet that is not different than the differences in practices that we see between the Schmiedeleut, Dariusleut, and Lehrerleut.[43]

What becomes apparent was that the traditionalist Hutterites felt strongly that the 'security of the church' lay in the members faithfully upholding the traditions and *Ordnungen* as expressed by the idiom: "*alte Marksteine soll man nicht verrücken* [ancient landmarks should never be moved]." In that context, the Bruderhof insist-

---

41 Balthasar Trumbi to Peter Hofer "Primavera an Die Hutterische Brüder Kirche [Primavera to the Church of the Hutterian Brethren]," 11 August 1951, in author's collection, translated. The Bruderhof leaders pointed out that coffee, tea, and tobacco were all considered unnecessary and were equally banned by the Hutterites in Wischinka. If the Hutterites were allowed to drink coffee and tea, both of which are also stimulates, why couldn't the Bruderhof members use tobacco?

42 According to Tony Waldner, the Bruderhof countered this by reminding the Hutterites that in the early years in North America, the Hutterites had also allowed women to participate in council meetings. An as yet unpublished Ordinance from 1877 states: "*Im Mei ist erkennt das alle getaufte Verheiratete (Glieder) im Rat zu nehmen, auch alle Jünglinge, wenn sie getauft sein u 20 Jahr alt sein, kennen sie auch im Rath genommen werden, u kennen sich auch nach der Älter setzen. Auch Jungfrauen. Doch nach belieben, wer will kann auch bei den Jungfrauen sitzen bleiben.* [In May it was discerned that all baptized married people (members) are to be taken in the council, even the young men, when they are baptized and 20 years old, can also be included and sit according to age. Also the young women, but only those who want to; that is, the young women who wish to, may remain seated."

43 Balthasar Trumbi to Peter Hofer, 11 August 1951, in author's collection, translated.

ence on "*Freiheit des Geistes* [Freedom in the Spirit]" was viewed as "fundamentally false, injurious…," even tantamount to "anarchy." How can you live without laws that maintain order?[44]

On the other hand, the Bruderhof felt that blind adherence to the *Ordnung* was stifling the true working of the Spirit. They were deeply offended by the Hutterite leaders' accusation of spiritual immaturity and the charge that they supported an "*ordnungslose* [undisciplined]" society. They tried to point out that pure compliance to *Ordnung* or laws had not stopped the "partisan spirits, injustice…and divisions"[45] from creeping into the Hutterite church. These are the real evils that ought to be rooted out of the church. They were committed to uphold matters concerning articles of faith, or *geistgewirkte Ordungen*, such as the Service of the Word [*Dienste*], marriage, baptism, the role of government, and pacifism. The inner unity of the Spirit was far more important than the concern for outer uniformity.

The Bruderhof leaders then turned the tables on the Hutterites and accused them of abandoning Hutterite articles of faith. For instance, during WWII the Hutterites had allowed their young men to work in alternative service camps. The Bruderhof leaders asked:

> In doing so, did you not give more to Caesar than Caesar is due? Was that not one of the reasons your forefathers left Russia? Also, in some cases, Hutterite community's paid money to the government so that their young men could work on farms instead of going into the military. Other communities are reported to have purchased war bonds. Yes, you do claim that you requested of the government that the money be used only to help those in need. But did you investigate whether they were doing so? If you did this, as you claim, out of love for the poor (and Jesus loves not only the poor who live in community but all the world's poor), you would have taken the opportunity to send out Brothers who

---

44 Ibid.
45 Author unknown. Informal meeting notes made at a minister's conference in James Valley, August 1955, in author's collection.

Five Hutterite carpenters helped build the Forest River House at Woodcrest Bruderhof. Left to right: Fred Kleinsasser (Sturgeon Creek, MB), Dave Waldner (Milltown, MB), Paul Maendel (Forest River, ND), Samuel Hofer (Bloomfield, MB), and Darius Maendel (Forest River, ND). [SOURCE: Jacob Kleinsasser Collection.]

could have used the money to help where there is actual need and so you would have been able to make a small beginning at mission. If you had sent out brothers on mission, they would have experienced that many people are not poor because they are lazy or alcoholics but rather that the world, in its unrighteousness, causes many innocent people to suffer, especially children.[46]

Other points of criticism raised by the Bruderhof leaders were in regards to *Eigennutz*, the earning of money for personal use at the expense of the community, as well as the fact that there were rich and poor Hutterite communities. This last point was of particular importance to the Bruderhof leaders who pointed out that their communities in both Paraguay and England had suffered extreme poverty and hardship on account of the war. At times, the Bruderhof members struggled to find necessities of food and shelter:

> Even at present [in Paraguay], we are, financially speaking, in poorer straights than any of your poor-

---

46   Balthasar Trumbi to Peter Hofer, 11 August 1951, in author's collection, translated.

est communities. During this time, our brothers and sisters often asked why our North American brethren don't send aid.[47]

Despite the tensions between the two groups, an uneasy unity remained. By 1954, things appeared to be improving as five Hutterite carpenters were sent to help with construction at Woodcrest. In letters that these brothers wrote, the Hutterites expressed their concern regarding adherence to the *Ordnungen* but also amazement at what they were experiencing. Samuel Hofer from Bloomfield most powerfully captures this in a letter he wrote to his brother in May of 1955:

> When people are dependent on God and not on written rules and regulation, their battle is fought by God, and we can almost sit back and watch the marvellous work of him performed before our eyes.[48]

Fred Kleinsasser from Sturgeon Creek wrote:

> I must say, that this is the most wonderful experience I ever had in my life, it is a real recreation. It is only now that I know and realize what John Maendel said and has told us, that when we once see the love and open hearts we will not notice the whiskers and black pants.[49]

However, despite this optimism, things soon took a turn for the worse. In July of 1955, a meeting took place in Chicago at the request of certain brothers from Forest River. Many Hutterites of that time had a deep longing for outreach and mission, and they saw in the Bruderhof—particularly in Woodcrest—the possibility of a revitalization of the vision for mission work, similar to that of 16th-century Hutterites. When members at Forest River requested help, families from Paraguay and Woodcrest were sent to live at Forest River. This dramatically increased the tension as a rift began to form within the community with Servant of the Word, Andreas

---

47 Ibid.
48 Sam Hofer to John Hofer, May 1955, in author's collection.
49 Fred Kleinsasser to Jacob Kleinsasser, May 1955, in author's collection.

David Decker, Jr., Starland, MN. [SOURCE: Jacob Kleinsasser Collection.]

Hofer and a small group on one side, and those in favour of aligning more closely with the Bruderhof on the other side. On August 29, 1955, the Schmiedeleut *Ältester*, Peter Hofer, sent eleven ministers to Forest River to mediate a solution. When the break-away group rejected the eleven Schmiedeleut ministers and treated them defiantly and disrespectfully, the Hutterite *Ältester* viewed this as an open rebellion and a hostile takeover. He wrote to all the Schmiedeleut communities:

> Herewith we declare that all those members of Forest River who are guilty of breaking their vows and who have fallen away are to be shunned....We the twenty-eight preachers who met in James Valley Bruderhof, are informing you that the represent-

atives of the Paraguay church should henceforth be shunned by all the churches in Canada and the United States. They will not be tolerated on any of our *Hofs*.[50]

Without a doubt, much of what transpired in Forest River reflected, to some extent, the internal struggle for power and dominance, which was taking place within the Bruderhof communities. Whatever the case may be, the Forest River conflict brought about a sudden and painful end to a relationship which started more than 20 years before when Eberhard Arnold came to North America and requested that his small group be united with the Hutterites. In Forest River, those members who still wanted to stay with the Hutterites had to pack their belongings and return to Manitoba where, together with New Rosedale Community, they established Fairholme Community in 1959.[51]

For many Hutterites, these early experiences with mission and outreach were profoundly unsettling and caused many to look upon potential new members with suspicion. Reflecting on this period in Hutterite history, David Decker, Jr. from Starland wrote:

> Mission is something that is only dreamed of by the most enthusiastic brothers and sisters. The majority don't want any new people to come into their communities as they see them only as liabilities. Various excuses are offered to try and justify their thinking. 'They won't be able to make it anyway! The road is much too tight for them to walk!' Or, 'They won't be able to accept or understand our traditions and customs and our Low German dialect is too hard to learn.' These and many other excuses are offered.[52]

Shortly after the breaking away from the Hutterite church, the Bruderhof communities in Paraguay were abandoned, and all the remaining members moved to the United States. Heini Arnold,

---

50 Peter Hofer to "Dear brothers" [all Schmiedeleut Hutterite communities], 6 September 1955, in author's collection.
51 This conflict has many layers. For instance, by the early 1970s, the Airport and Pine Creek communities also came into existence as a result.
52 David Decker, Jr. to "all concerned," 17 May 1993, in author's collection.

Eberhard's son, was elected elder despite the arguments of some that it was not right for another Arnold to take the position.

In New York, Woodcrest became the center for the Bruderhof movement. Many new people joined the Bruderhof communities, and the movement found new life. The communities in Paraguay had gone through a transformation which saw it depart from Eberhard's vision for the church, placing more emphasis on community life than on a transformed life. However, with Heini Arnold as elder, a rebirth of Eberhard's vision was possible.

This concludes lecture two. We have followed the struggle of the Schmiedeleut and Bruderhof communities as they developed individual identities shaped, in many ways, by the socioeconomic and political environments that surrounded them. In the concluding lecture, we will pick up the story in 1973–1974. The uniting between the Bruderhof and Hutterite communities was a pivotal moment in Hutterite history. It seemed to herald a time of renewal and growth, but at the same time, seeds of discord were inadvertently planted.

LECTURE THREE
1974: The "Year of Jubilee"

The 1974 uniting between the Schmiedeleut and Bruderhof communities was a pivotal moment for both the Hutterite and Bruderhof movements. In 1964, Bruderhof elder, Heinrich [Heini] Arnold, and several other Bruderhof Servants of the Word visited the Hutterites in Manitoba. At that time, *Ältester* Peter Hofer's health was already failing, and Heini Arnold especially wanted to apologize to him personally for what happened in Forest River. After a short meeting with the three Bruderhof members, Peter Hofer told Heini Arnold that he personally forgave him for anything he might have done. The next day, Peter Hofer convened a small meeting in Milltown, Manitoba where Heini Arnold again apologized to the 17 ministers who were in attendance. He was again assured that he was forgiven.

The reconciliation that took place in 1964, did not, however, lead to a uniting between the Hutterites and the Bruderhof communities. As in 1955, there were strong differences in cultural and spiritual practises that existed between the two groups. Bruderhof married men were not required to wear beards and their women did not wear head coverings. The Bruderhof had completely abandoned the Hutterite dress code. As in 1955, the Bruderhof allowed the use of musical instruments, performed dramas and celebrated certain events with folk dances. For many traditional-minded Hutterites, these were almost impossible hurdles to overcome. Despite these differences, there was a deep longing on both sides for a reuniting.

In 1973, Jacob Kleinsasser (Crystal Spring) and Jacob Hofer (Elm River, later Valley View) paid the Bruderhof a surprise visit while on a trip to Ottawa regarding church business. During their brief stay, the two Hutterite ministers were deeply moved by their experience. They both felt strongly that a uniting should be possible. In June of that same year, three Dariusleut ministers also visited the Bruderhof communities, one of them being Peter Tschetter from Mixburn, AB. These Hutterite ministers also felt a deep longing for a reuniting with the Bruderhof.

On the Bruderhof side, there were still strong concerns that a uniting with the Hutterites would force them to comply with the Hutterite traditions and *Ordnungen*. The question of adopting the Hutterite dress code, particularly the head covering for women, was of particular concern. For his part, Heini Arnold shared these concerns, but he also longed for deeper unity between the Hutterites:

> I for my part want by no means to force anything, but the brothers in the West simply won't understand it if we are not willing to yield to them on some points out of love.[1]

Many Hutterites also feared a uniting with the Bruderhof as "they did not know what would be brought into their midst" with the influx of such a large group of non-ethnic Hutterites. Would the Bruderhof be a 'worldly influence' which would lead many young Hutterites away from the church?[2]

Because of these fears, many spoke out against any form of uniting. However, other ministers like Jacob Kleinsasser from Crystal Spring, and David Waldner and Michael Waldner from Milltown "pleaded with many who were opposed [to] reserve judgment until you have heard the [Bruderhof] brothers speak."[3]

Because of the ban placed upon the Bruderhof by the Hutterites, the groups could not worship together. In 1973, a small group of Hutterites, including *Ältester* Joseph Kleinsasser from Sunnyside, visited the Bruderhof communities. Jacob Kleinsasser spoke out sharply against this prohibition of worshipping together saying,

---

1 Merrill Mow, *Torches Rekindled*, 206–207.
2 Ibid., 208.
3 Ibid.

An artist's rendition of the uniting between the Bruderhof and Hutterites at Sturgeon Creek, Manitoba. Heini Arnold is greeted by *Ältester* Joseph Kleinsasser while he is embracing Jacob Kleinsasser. [SOURCE: Merrill Mow, *Torches Rekindled*, 219.]

> I don't understand one point. If there is ever a reason for coming to prayer, to lying prostrate before God crying for help, and [if] both sides have the same longing, why [there] should be a hindrance.[4]

Heini Arnold then stood up and spoke in a loud voice, "This is the hour when we shall come to prayer."[5] The moment when the two sides came together in prayer proved to be a significant moment in the history of both groups.

In 1974, at a meeting in Sturgeon Creek, the concerns on both sides seemed to melt away. Those who were present at that meeting spoke of how God's spirit stepped in and overwhelmed all those present. As Jacob Kleinsasser put it, "If Jesus [comes] into the center, everything will fall in place and that is the only way to achieve unity."[6]

---

4 Bruderhof. "Of one Mind: The Bruderhof Relationship to the Hutterian Brethren, Part 2," YouTube Video, 3:09. This video is no longer available on YouTube; in author's collection.
5 Ibid., 2:36.
6 Ibid., 3:51.

At the conclusion of the 1974 uniting meeting, the gathered ministers decided that all the baptized brothers and sisters who had left Forest River would need to be placed in exclusion for a time because of their behaviour in Forest River and the fact that they left the Hutterite church. Five Hutterite ministers would visit the Bruderhof communities to carry out the exclusion and forgiveness process; this would once again make them members of the Hutterite Church. This last point came as a great surprise to the Bruderhof. Heini Arnold wrote of this saying,

> We had no opportunity to talk together alone, but we all felt that it was God's leading and that we had nothing to say. It would have been a second Forest River-type sin if we had said we couldn't do that without asking at home first.[7]

Peter Tschetter, one of the Dariusleut representatives present at the meeting later wrote to his friend, minister Samuel Kleinsasser[8] from Sturgeon Creek, saying,

> Does this not represent for us the hundredth year, yes, the year of jubilee…, a forgiving year, a year of reconciliation, when both the slave and the master have their hearts guided by God's goodness, and have been united to a new year, a new life…. For this I cannot raise my hands enough. A figure of one thousand people added to the church. A whole people…this was accomplished by God![9]

It is important to acknowledge that the concerns from both sides were still lurking under the surface. At the time of the uniting, both groups were able to lay aside their differences in an attempt to bring about a unity of spirit. However, there were also some unintended consequences which already sowed seeds of disunity from the very beginning. For instance, when the Bruderhof and Hutterites parted ways in 1955, the issues that separated them revolved around compliance with Hutterite customs and traditions.

---

7   Merrill Mow, *Torches Rekindled*, 217.
8   Kleinsasser was among those who strongly opposed the uniting. His father was the Samuel Kleinsasser who visited the Bruderhof in Paraguay in 1950.
9   Peter J. Tschetter to Samuel Kleinsasser, 13 January 1974, in author's collection.

Hutterite Ministers singing in Woodcrest, 1974. Left to right: *Ältester* Joseph Kleinsasser (Sunnyside, MB), Jacob Kleinsasser (Crystal Spring, MB), Jacob Hofer (Elm River, MB [later Valley View, MB]), 1974. [SOURCE: Jacob Kleinsasser Collection.]

In 1974, Heini Arnold and the Bruderhof representatives were told that the Hutterites would no longer ask the Bruderhof to adopt the traditions and customs of the Hutterian church.[10] It was decided that it was enough if they lived according to the leading of Christ's spirit.[11] However, when we look closely at the narrative, we can see that those concerns were still there. Heini Arnold wrote,

> In Crystal Spring, we from the East talked together very briefly, and all felt convicted that it would have been a great sin if we had not accepted. We would once again have sinned against the Hutterite Brothers and would again have had to ask for forgiveness.[12]

He then recounts how someone asked about the "points" or *Ordnungen* and that Jacob Kleinsasser had stated that he and *Ältester* Joseph Kleinsasser "had quite intentionally not brought up the

---

10   Merrill Mow, *Torches Rekindled*, 220.
11   David Decker, Jr. to "all concerned," 17 May 1993, in author's collection.
12   Merrill Mow, *Torches Rekindled*, 220.

Ältester **Joseph Kleinsasser in Woodcrest, 1974.** [SOURCE: Jacob Kleinsasser Collection.]

points so as not to bring dissension."[13] The remainder of the letter indicates that Arnold felt uneasy about the implications this openendedness would have for the future relationship.

What complicated the matter even more was that the Bruderhof did not expect the Hutterites to take them back as members of the Hutterite Church. Heini and the other Bruderhof leaders who attended the Sturgeon Creek meetings were faced with the awkward position of having to return home and telling their people that they were now Hutterites again. The issue of the exclusion for all baptized members who left Forest River was particularly thorny as many of them seemed to feel, even years later, that the exclusion was wrong. According to one source, when Heini returned home, he ran into serious opposition to the uniting, especially regarding the adoption of the Hutterite dress code, and particularly head coverings for the women. In the end, Heini Arnold pushed for the total adoption of the Hutterite dress code as he felt that without it, there would never be a real unity between the two groups. After Heini Arnold passed away in 1982, and intermarriages between the Hutterites and the Bruderhof took place, these tensions began to grow as some Hutterite leaders began to demand that the Brud-

---

13   Ibid.

Ian Kleinsasser

Interaction with the Bruderhof manifested positive elements in Hutterite communities such as the joyful participation in communal events. [SOURCE: Author's collection.]

erhof once again fully adopt the Hutterite orders and customs. The differences in childhood education, acceptance of musical instruments, social activism, and differing worship practises began to drive a wedge between some Hutterite communities and the Bruderhof. For many Bruderhof members, the Hutterite dress code became a form of social oppression.

However, years of interaction and intermarriage also produced many positive results. Those Schmiedeleut communities which interacted most with the Bruderhof were often transformed by this relationship. Bruderhof members who moved to Hutterite communities for extended periods brought with them a love for nature, music, and social activism (e.g. prison ministry). Probably one of the most profound and lasting impacts of the Bruderhof relationship was that it reawakened in many Hutterites a deeper appreciation for communal living. Many Hutterite youths who visited the Bruderhof communities were deeply moved by the element of joy and simplicity of life that permeated Bruderhof society. They began to see their own traditions as a hindrance to authentic communal living. In contrast to the high standard of living found among many Hutterite communities, the Bruderhof communities lived a much simpler life, particularly regarding housing. While our communities were becoming more autonomous or individualistic, the

Bruderhof communities strove to maintain a deeper level of unity among their communities.

Hutterite Church Corporation

Beginning around 1960, the Hutterite Church Corporation faced two major challenges: First, matters relating to income tax and secondly, the Canada Pension Plan (CPP) issues. Hutterites have always believed that it is their responsibility to pay taxes with one exception, namely when taxes are specifically levied for war purposes. Since settling in Canada, Hutterites have consistently paid their local or municipal taxes. However, when it came to paying income tax, which was a War Measures Act tax and a federal tax, the Hutterites had a problem as the federal tax

> assumed that people had individual income. To the Hutterites the idea of an individual income, like that of private property, was in fundamental conflict with their religion.[14]

Income Tax

Before 1960, the Hutterite did not have to worry about income tax because their communities were viewed as a church and, as such, paid no income tax. This was, in part, because of the vow of perpetual poverty every Hutterite makes when formally joining the church at baptism. Additionally, because Hutterites did not have individual income, the government did not know how the income tax would be levied against them. Moreover, prior to the 1960s, the income of the average Hutterite community was so low that no significant amount of revenue would be gained even if a satisfactory way of levying the tax was found. That this was a growing concern among Hutterite leaders and their legal counsel, can be demonstrated by their initial refusal to accept Family Allowance and Old Age Pension on the advice of their legal counsel, Ernest Fletcher. He had advised them that their continuing refusal to accept Family Allowance and Old Age Pensions would help remove suspicion that they were 'getting something for nothing,' and help insure that the Revenue Department would leave them alone. This attempt by

---

14   Unknown, "Income Tax and the Hutterites," in author's collection.

Lester B. Pearson and Maryon Pearson with a group of Hutterite ladies in Winkler, Manitoba on October 7, 1965. [SOURCE: PC 18, A.81-12, Winnipeg Tribune Personalities Collection, Winnipeg Tribune fonds, University of Manitoba Archives & Special Collections, Winnipeg, Manitoba, Canada.]

the Hutterites to avoid criticism from the general public did not work. Public criticism of the Hutterites eventually prompted the federal government to announce late in the 1960s that it would look into the matter further with the intent of taxing the Hutterites in a way that would produce a tax "relatively equivalent to that paid by similar farming operations" and be "clearly supported by law."[15]

At this point, the government also indicated that, as most of the Hutterite communities were incorporated, they might be subject to a corporate tax. This was a huge concern for the Hutterite communities. A corporate tax would be extremely heavy and could bankrupt many of the Hutterite communities. Ever since the 1930s, most of the Hutterite communities had been incorporated. As we saw in the first lecture, this came about largely because of Barrickman's financial difficulties. At that time, Barrickman had successfully argued that they were a farming operation as well as a religious organization and were thus allowed to claim protection

---

15   Ibid.

under the Farmers Aid Protection Program. This was a short-term win for Barrickman, but a long-term loss for the Hutterite church.

Early in 1963, assessments were made of two incorporated Hutterite communities. Legal counsel for the Hutterites filed a formal objection and was able to delay the decision for a few years, but by 1965, the objection was overruled.

At this point the lawyers for the Hutterites met with the Minister of the Revenue Department and requested a negotiated settlement which would be on a basis other than corporate tax. At the same time, the Hutterites wanted to keep the issue out of the courts. They argued that even a court ruling favourable to the government might have such a far-reaching implication that it would be to the advantage of the government to work out a negotiated settlement. The late *Ältester* Jacob Kleinsasser recounted that they told the Minister that if the government assessed a corporate tax against the Hutterites, they would have their members all file for unemployment insurance during the winter months, as this was a time when most Hutterites were out of work. The government agreed to enter into negotiations. After lengthy negotiations, an agreement was reached. The Hutterites made a significant concession by accepting an arrangement which carried the appearance of Hutterites receiving an individual income. The Hutterites agreed to take the total income of a community, divide it by the number of members, make the appropriate deductions, and then repost income tax accordingly.

Even though the Hutterites agreed to pay income tax in accordance with the terms of the agreement, they did not want to be part of the Canada Pension Plan. At the beginning of the negotiations, which took place in Winnipeg, a government official assured Roy Baker, legal counsel for the Hutterites, that "…under the Canada Pension Plan, the Hutterites…in view of their vow of perpetual poverty and the fact that no cash income is received, by any one of them, they are exempt."[16] Later the government backtracked on this promise and said that they could not exclude the Hutterites from CPP; however, they also stated that the agreement would not "affect the possibility of Colonies approaching the Government in

---

16 James A. Robb to G. W. Ainslie, 6 January 1967, in author's collection.

order to obtain a revision in Legislation" of the Canada Pension Plan.[17] The Hutterites agreed to settle the income tax issue in spite of this uncertainty about the pension problem. They decided that they would have their lawyers work on the pension issue as soon as the income tax problem was settled. In 1968, the Schmiedeleut and the Lehrerleut groups signed the agreement.

The Dariusleut, however, did not agree to sign. The government assumed that the Dariusleut group would eventually fall in line with the other two groups, and proceeded to make assessments and to levy taxes on all Hutterite communities according to the terms of the agreement. The Dariusleut, instead of paying the taxes, launched an appeal to have the assessment set aside. This led to a long drawn-out litigation battle. On February 16, 1972, the federal government won the first round of litigation. Nearly two years later, on the 19th of November, the Federal Court Trial Division also ruled in favour of the government. The Dariusleut appealed to the Federal Court, Appeal Division. This became a major turning point. The ruling, on appeal, was in favour of the Hutterites and found that Hutterites did not have a taxable income. The Government launched an appeal to the Supreme Court of Canada. However, on February 11, 1976, the Supreme Court dismissed the appeal stating simply, "We agree with the judgment of the Federal Court of Appeal...."[18]

This turn of events had very serious implications for the Government and also for the Schmiedeleut and Lehrerleut who had been paying taxes ever since the 1968 agreement. The agreement which they had worked out with the Government in 1968 was now no longer valid. It raised several important questions: First, would the Schmiedeleut and Lehrerleut receive a refund? Second, would all the Hutterite communities now be taxed as corporations or trusts and end up paying substantially more than what the agreement had obligated them to pay? Third, would it be possible in some way to retain the basic principles of the agreement in some other form?

It did not take the Federal Government long to make a decision. The Government would assess the Dariusleut as a corporation. The

---

17 Ibid.
18 The Queen vs. Joseph K. Wipf et all, 57 (Canadian Tax Court 1976).

Schmiedeleut and Lehrerleut would continue paying taxes on the same basis as they had been since 1969. The Dariusleut appealed the ruling but lost. The judgment was devastating for the Dariusleut. There were 88 Dariusleut communities, all of whom would be bound by the judgement of this case. The total sum which the government initially tried to collect from them was said to amount to 37 million dollars.

This conflict, though it started with the Hutterites working together to negotiate a tax agreement with the Federal Government, soon caused a deep rift to develop between the three groups. The Dariusleut leaders accused the Schmiedeleut and Lehrerleut of paying war taxes (blood money).[19] The Dariusleut continued to fight the Federal Government but ultimately lost their appeal. In the end, they were given the option to either accept the ruling and be taxed as a corporation or sign on to the same tax agreement as the Schmiedeleut and Lehrerleut. Grudgingly, they joined the other two *Leut*, but resentment lingered.

Canada Pension Plan (CPP)

In 1965 the Canadian Government introduced the Canada Pension Plan and in 1966, the Government began collecting the pension premiums. The Canada Pension Plan was considered as an important milestone in Canadian social development. It was designed to help people make financial provisions for their retirement and to protect themselves and their dependents or survivors against loss of income in the event of disability and death. The Hutterites and several small Mennonite groups opposed the Plan as they felt that such a program would "have the effect of diverting loyalty from the church to dependence upon the government and supplant a vital and important function of the Church."[20]

---

19 Income Tax was brought into effect during WWI under the War Measures Act. During the war, taxes were levied on luxury items such as alcohol and tobaccos. Towards the end of the war, the government introduced a goods and service tax. Shortly thereafter the Dominion Government moved to tax the incomes of businesses. The Business Profits War Tax Act of 1916 required all Canadian corporations having $50,000, or more, in capital to file a yearly tax return. Personal income tax, introduced under the Income War Tax Act of 1917, was conceived—like the other wartime taxes—as a temporary measure.

20 "The Hutterite Church of Canada Basis of Objection to Government Sponsored Social Security Programs," 6 January 1967, in author's collection.

Early in 1969, Hutterites began to express their objections regarding participation in the Canada Pension Plan. They had not raised any prior objection to the Plan as they were in the process of negotiating the Income Tax settlement with the Government. Up until 1969, the Hutterites had not paid any Income Tax and thus the Canada Pensions Plan did not apply to them. As part of the Income Tax agreement, the Hutterites reluctantly agreed to allow the arrangement whereby they would be dividing their total income by the number of members. Nevertheless, they agreed to the arrangement for income tax purposes only. They argued that

> we view and hold that the Understanding of Agreement reached with [the] Department to tax [Hutterite] members on an individual basis, is a concession on our part in the spirit of public cooperation and tolerance only.[21]

Additionally, the Hutterites had received assurance that they were "making this agreement without prejudice to the rights of the Colonies to contest their liability to pay into the Canada Pension Fund."[22] Now, the Government insisted that the Canada Pension Plan was all-inclusive and that the Hutterites and Mennonites had to pay into the program. The only way Hutterites could get out of this obligation was if the government agreed to legislative changes exempting them.

The Hutterites argued that by forcing them to pay into and accept Canada Pension Funds, the Canadian Government was violating a promise made to them when they first immigrated to Canada. In 1899, James A. Smart, then Deputy Minister of the Department of the Interior, stated that

> there will be no interference with their living as a Commonwealth if they desire to do so…The members of the Society in question may rest assured that the statements made as above are of as full value

---

21 Jacob J. Waldner (for the Hutterite Brethren Church, Lehrerleut Group) to Jean-Pierre Cote, Minister of National Revenue, April 20, 1970, in author's collection.

22 "Exemption from the Canada Pension Plan," an unattributed brief submitted to the Canadian government, possibly by attorney Roy Baker, ca. 1978, in author's collection.

to them as they could be made by an Order of the Government in Council or any document of that nature.[23]

The Hutterites said they now understood this to be "a continuing moral commitment entitling them to the privilege of exemption from the Canada Pension Plan which interfered with their living as a commonwealth."[24]

Even though the Hutterites received support for their cause from a variety of different public persons, their request for exemption was ultimately denied. The government

> argued that to exempt [the Hutterites] would create serious problems for young people and others who did not want to continue in these sects. It was pointed out that the leaders of these groups strive continuously to maintain their communities against 'worldly' temptations, even to the point of objecting to high school education.[25]

Helping the Hutterites, in this case, would only help them maintain their system and thus slow the process of assimilation.

The Canada Pension Plan issue dragged out for eight years before a mutually agreeable settlement was reached. Even though the Hutterites continued to lobby the government, it was the Mennonites of Ontario who finally made the breakthrough that resulted in a favourable agreement for Old Order Mennonites and Hutterites. This came about largely through the work of Conservative Member of Parliament Herb Gray, who, incidentally, was Canada's first Jewish cabinet minister. After meeting with and carefully listening to the Mennonites' request, Gray agreed to bring the issue to Cabinet for further discussion. Herb Gray was, according to the Mennonite leaders, "the first person to give serious consideration to the religious aspect of the problem."[26] Less then two weeks later, the Government announced that it would bring in an amendment

---

23 Jason A. Smart to W. F. McCreary, 1899, in author's collection.
24 Unknown, "Income Tax and the Hutterites," in author's collection, 23.
25 Ibid., 25–26.
26 Ibid., 32.

to the Canada Pension Plan to accommodate both the Old Order Mennonites and Hutterites. After one more round of debate in the House of Commons, the provision granting exemption was passed on the 7th of November, 1974.[27]

There are several important lessons to be learned from this process. First, is the recognition of the inherent tension that exists between religious groups such as the Hutterites and the state within which they exist. The identity and internal dynamics of each group will invariably lead to some form of conflict. As Hutterites, we often view these conflicts as 'persecution' by the state. Seeing every stumbling block as a form of religious persecution is, in my estimation, extremely unwise. Instead, we must recognize that in any healthy multicultural society, tension will occasionally arise between various groups that need to be worked out.

A second lesson we can learn is the enormous lobbying effort put forth by Hutterite leaders. They were unwilling to accept the negative responses as final. They did not seek publicity. They did not try to 'embarrass' the government. But they were unshakable in their position and in their belief that the government would eventually see the rightness of their plea.

Finally, as Hutterites we need to gratefully acknowledge the fact that the Canadian state eventually did extend a degree of accommodation to our forebearers in allowing us to live as communities somewhat separated from the larger Canadian society.

---

27 When CPP was introduced in 1969, the Hutterites agreed to pay the required premiums, albeit under protest. During the conflict, they stopped making payments (1966–1971). At the time of settlement, the government made it clear that the legislation would not be retroactive prior to 1st of January, 1972. Over the years from 1972 to 1978, outstanding CPP premiums were reduced by the application of various refunds payable to the individual members and by applying community tax payments otherwise than instructed by the Hutterite communities. On a number of occasions, the Hutterites objected to the payment of these premiums. In 1977 an Order in Council was passed by the Government allowing for the cancellation of outstanding Canada Pension premiums and interest. In 1978 the Hutterite communities were notified that legal problems had arisen that prevented the completion of the remissions. Also, a great number of 1978 Manitoba Property Tax Credit refunds and Manitoba Cost of Living Credit refunds were again applied to the outstanding Canada Pension balances.

The On-Going Struggle for Education

When the Hutterites immigrated to Canada, they came with the understanding that they would be able to have their own schools where Hutterite educators worked with Hutterite children. However, upon settling in Canada, the Hutterites soon discovered that they would have to send their children to public schools. All instruction would be in English and teachers would be hired by the local school boards. It astonishes me to no end that our people simply accepted this situation without putting up a fight. In part we can blame the social and economic upheaval that the Hutterites experienced during World War 1 and the subsequent move to Canada. Because of their hasty departure from the USA, the Hutterites suffered significant financial losses. As a result, they had to work extremely hard to earn a living.

During the Great Depression of the 1930s, Hutterite communities, along with the rest of North America, struggled to have enough to eat. As a result, very few new communities were built. Some even went bankrupt. The Depression years ended when World War II began. This brought on new problems as the communities were called upon to support the war efforts by having their young men enlist in alternative service camps.

In light of these hardships, it is somewhat understandable—but not excusable—that the Hutterites neglected the education of their children.

Such was the situation in Hutterite communities well into the 20th-century. The time when Hutterite teachers taught in Hutterite schools was all but forgotten. However, an ever-dwindling number of elderly Hutterites never gave up hoping that someday this would again become the reality. It was this older generation who lamented the current situation and kept the spark of hope alive which was needed to once again light the fire which had all but been extinguished.

Every great movement needs a catalyst to get it started. So, what was the catalyst which finally led to the training of the first Hutterite teachers? One likely reason was the system of permit teaching which was developed as a way to deal with the war-time shortage of teachers (1941–1945).[28] Under this system, anyone who wanted to try teaching could receive a teaching license. Many of these teaching candidates had received six weeks of preparation at the United College in Winnipeg, but some arrived at their schools with no formal training. As one can imagine, for many of these teachers, the task proved to be too difficult. As a result, some Hutterite communities would go through three to four teachers in one school term. One such Hutterite school was Fairholme School.

Jacob D. Maendel, minister of Fairholme Community, became increasingly frustrated with this situation. In the early 1960s, he encouraged his brother, Peter Maendel to take the required training to become a certified teacher. Peter completed his studies in 1962 and was eventually followed by five other Hutterites: Elias Kleinsasser, Crystal Spring (1970), David Kleinsasser, Crystal Spring (1980), Dora Maendel, Fairholme (1985), Anna Maendel, Fairholme (1985), and Hilda Maendel, New Rosedale (1991).

In 1995, a new wave of Hutterite educators began their formal training through the Brandon University Hutterite Education Program (BUHEP). With this program, Brandon University provided instruction to Hutterian students in both on-campus and on-community settings. During its years of existence, the BUHEP program saw approximately 75 Hutterite educators receive their teaching degrees.[29]

Hutterite educators of today, however, face many challenges. While English is rapidly becoming our dominant language, few Hutterites speak it with the fluency of a native English-speaker. This is not surprising as we live in an English-speaking country and are constantly exposed to more and more English. Additionally, we have greatly neglected the training of our German school teachers and as a result, German has declined to such a level that many Hutterites are not conversant in their mother-tongue. As a supposed bilingual people, we are now confronted with the reality that we are not truly proficient in either language.

---

28 Sheila Grover, *Winnipeg Schools: A Thematic Study of the Modern Period, 1945–1975* (Winnipeg: Winnipeg Architecture Foundation, 2012), 52–53.

29 The program formally folded in the mid-2000s. A strong relationship between the Hutterite community and Brandon University, including the maintenance of a scholarship fund for Hutterite students, still remains.

Another major challenge is the prevailing attitude that education is unimportant. Expressions such as "*Je gelehrter, je verkehrter* [More learned, more perverted]" support the misconception that our foreparents thought and taught that higher education was unnecessary and even wrong. However, the Hutterite sermons, chronicles, confessions of faith, and other literature were not produced by uneducated or uncultured people. Instead, they demonstrate that, even though our Hutterite ancestors objected to 'worldly' education, they developed their own system of education which even exceeded the standards of mainstream society in notable ways. As a group, we must wrestle with the question of how a people who were once renowned for the advances in their education system, have allowed it to fall into serious neglect. How have we come to such a place and time where it is even considered wrong by some Hutterites, to have our own teachers teaching in our schools? As we move forward, I hope that the seeds planted by leaders like Jacob D. Maendel and Peter Maendel will continue to grow so that we are able to create an education system which will equip our children to cultivate Hutterite society so it flourishes as it seeks to witness to the kingdom of God.

Decades of Conflict:
Looking Back, While Moving Forward

There is nothing more difficult than writing about conflict. This is especially true when you find yourself entrenched in the very conflict you are trying to write about, yet this is where I find myself. The 1960s, and even more so, the 1970s, were a time of tremendous changes for Hutterites. As I have attempted to show in the last two lectures, the Hutterite church, in particular, the Schmiedeleut Conference, faced many challenges and changes. The study of history demonstrates that anytime changes are introduced into a society, they invariably cause anxiety, concern and even hostility. The reality of many of these conflicts is that the people who are caught up in them are unaware of the root causes which have brought their particular group or society to this point of crisis. This conundrum, I believe, is true in our present context as well. In this final section, I will try to look at some of the key areas of conflict which led to the church schism or break of 1992. We will look at

Ältester Peter Hofer, James Valley, Manitoba, 1964.
[SOURCE: *Treasures of Time* Collection, HBBC Digital Collection.]

some of the key points of tension without going into a great deal of detail. We will conclude by considering whether it is possible to imagine a hopeful future.

American vs. Canadian: The Struggle for Church Leadership

During the 1960s, strong tensions within the Hutterite church began to manifest themselves between some of the American and Canadian communities. Oral histories and personal correspondence between *Ältester* Joseph Kleinsasser from Sunnyside and key American Schmiedeleut leaders show that there was growing resentment among the American communities towards the church's office of the elder which was located in Canada since the eldership was revived in 1934. The lack of high-speed transportation and sparse availability of telephone technology meant that the community leaders had to rely mainly on the postal service to communicate. In that era, all major issues or decisions had to be made by a majority vote of all the ministers or, in some cases, all voting members of each community. For example, when problems arose within the American communities, they were relayed in writing to the *Ältester* in Manitoba. If necessary, the *Ältester* would then write to all the Schmiedeleut communities asking them to discuss and vote on the issue. The responses were tallied and returned to the *Ältester* who then sent the answer, in writing, to the American Schmiedeleut communities. This created a significant delay in the process, and the American communities felt that their concerns were being inadequately addressed. The American ministers pushed *Ältester* Peter Hofer to appoint an assistant to the *Ältester* from South Dakota.

The Church eventually agreed, and in 1962 Peter Hofer had selected Joseph Hofer[30] from Maxwell, SD, as the first American assistant to the *Ältester*. However, by doing so, the church soon found itself in a power struggle. When Joseph Hofer fell ill and couldn't carry out his duties, a small group of American Schmiedeleut ministers appointed a new assistant *Ältester* without consulting the new Manitoba *Ältester*, Joseph Kleinsasser from Sunnyside, MB. They installed Joseph Wipf from Plainview, SD, as his American counterpart.[31] When Joseph Kleinsasser heard about this, he and the Manitoba ministers requested that those responsible come to Manitoba for a hearing. After discussing the issue, the Manitoban leadership and ministers decided to put the incident behind them, but Joseph Wipf from Plainview community had to apologize publicly to the *Ältester* and the other Manitoba ministers. In a show of good faith, Joseph Kleinsasser then appointed Joseph Wipf to be the new South Dakota assistant. The increase in tensions between the American and Canadian Schmiedeleut conferences demonstrates the formation of an ideological divide which began to manifest itself within not only the Schmiedeleut Conference, but also the Darius- and Lehrerleut conferences as well. Both also have communities located on either side of the border and also deal with

---

30   Also known as Singer Vetter.
31   David Decker, Jr. to "all concerned," 17 May 1993, in author's collection.

noticeable tension between the American and Canadian communities.[32]

Ideological Disunity

During this time, and particularly during the eldership of Joseph Kleinsasser from Sunnyside, further tensions began to develop between Hutterite leaders regarding contrasting visions for the Hutterite church. Traditionalist leaders felt that by maintaining the traditions and ordinances of ancestors, they were honouring their memory and sacrifice. "Do not remove the *Markstein* [milestones]!" or "We need to hold fast to what we have!" were their watch cries. *Ältester* Joseph Kleinsasser and other ministers felt that the church had largely failed to live up to the example of the early Hutterites who, among other exemplary initiatives, sent out missionaries in accordance with Jesus' teachings.[33] These two conflicting visions came to a head in 1977.

In 1977, a year before he passed away, Joseph Kleinsasser refused to call the annual conference of the Schmiedeleut. Joseph Wipf from Plainview, SD, demanded to know why he dared cancel the yearly conference. The *Ältester* replied,

> I believe that our heavenly Father has very little pleasure in such meetings where very little godly conversation takes place, but mostly temporal or practical matters are discussed or dealt with. In contrast, our Saviour's last command to his disciples (Matthew 28:19) is completely disregarded. 'For my people have committed two evils: they have forsaken Me, the fountain of living waters, and hewed out cisterns for themselves, broken cisterns, that can hold no water (Jeremiah 2:3).'[34]

> What are these wells which are full of holes and can hold no water? These are human vanity and accomplishments which barely last a year. These things

---

32 Cf. Joe Wurtz and Danny Gross. *Washington Tagebuch, January 18–24, 2010.* Published by authors, 2010.
33 Cf. Matthew 28:19.
34 Joseph Kleinsasser to Joseph Wipf, 29 September 1977, in author's collection.

are worthless when it comes to establishing peace and unity.[35]

In 1978, the same year he passed away, *Ältester* Joseph Kleinsasser addressed a church gathering in Sunnyside with a lamentation from Jeremiah 11:13: "For your gods have become as many as your towns, O Judah; and as many as the streets of Jerusalem." He then asked,

> Is this also true among the Hutterite brotherhoods and communities? For one seeks righteousness with a collar on a jacket; if you do not have one or have a different one than I, then I will not recognize you as a Christian. The other says, if you have pants with a crooked zipper, or if you do not have the same kind of hat that I have, you are going toward perdition and mock your salvation. Such imaginings abound as if our salvation were to be found in mere rags. Why don't such think instead about what the apostle Paul wrote to the Roman church (6:23): 'For the wages of sin is death, but the gift of God is eternal life in Christ Jesus our Lord.' Those who hold to these things, rob Jesus Christ of the honour that He alone deserves and try to honour themselves.[36]

What these struggles demonstrate is the growing tension within the Schmiedeleut church over competing visions of the direction the Hutterites ought to go.

A New *Ältester*

When *Ältester* Joseph Kleinsasser passed away in 1978, his assistant, Jacob Kleinsasser from Crystal Spring, was elected as the new *Ältester*. In the preceding decade, Jacob Kleinsasser had become increasingly involved in managing church organizations, particularly the Hutterite Church Corporation and the fight for equity and justice for Hutterite people. He was a key figure in the development

---

35   Joseph Kleinsasser, "Lament for the Hutterite People," 1978, in author's collection.
36   Ibid.

Ältester Joseph Kleinsasser and Jacob Kleinsasser, 1977.
[SOURCE: Jacob Kleinsasser Collection.]

of the 1950s Constitution, and he negotiated extensively with the provincial and federal governments regarding land restrictions, education, and taxation. As an *Ältester*, he had a strong vision for the church and an equally strong personality and leadership style which often forced underlying issues out into the open. Like Joseph Kleinsasser before him, Jacob Kleinsasser set out to reform the Schmiedeleut Conference which faced many societal and financial troubles. Where past annual Schmiedeleut Conferences had dealt mainly with establishing and maintaining *Ordnungen*, the new *Ältester* began to raise other concerns. For instance, he advocated for improved baptismal instruction to cultivate spiritual development versus the accepted '*schöne Älter*'[37] for those requesting baptism. He emphasized prudence, chastity and temperance within courtship to address loose dating practises and sexual immorality among Hut-

---

37 "Good age" or "appropriate age," is a phrase commonly used to communicate the attitude that age was a sufficient indicator of a person's preparedness for baptism.

terite youth. Describing the state of the church at this time, David Decker, Jr. (Starland, MN) wrote,

> The greatest evil creeping into the colonies, and the sickness of all humanity from the beginning of history was sexual impurity. The elder in 1974 and later our present elder Jacob Kleinsasser inherited a sick church community…. [The elder] immediately went to the task of cleaning up the mess, for, without cleansing we were headed for destruction. Illegitimate births were quadrupling, and no end was in sight. Many meetings were called to stop the fire out of control.[38]

Many people, including leaders, however, did not accept the *Ältester's* attempts to bring about spiritual reform.

At the same time as he was trying to bring about spiritual reform, *Ältester* Jacob Kleinsasser and other Schmiedeleut ministers were actively looking to find solutions to help financially struggling Schmiedeleut communities. After consultation with church financial advisors and the larger church, new credit, trust, mutual insurance, and medical companies were formed. To understand why these organizations were necessary, it is helpful to understand the economic context in which they developed.

In the 1980s and 90s, the Schmiedeleut Conference faced significant financial difficulties. Since moving to Manitoba in 1918, some of the Schmiedeleut communities had struggled financially because of huge mortgages and loans incurred from buying land at high prices. By the 1950s, however, the Hutterites had benefited from an upswing in the world economy, a period of prosperity that lasted until the early 1970s. During this time, many of the Hutterite communities began to spend more money than they could afford.[39] According to Hans Decker from Wolf Creek, SD, this increased focus on earning money had a severely detrimental impact on Hutterite education. Children were pulled from school as soon as possible so that they could begin to earn money. Brothers who

---

38   David Decker, Jr. to "all concerned," 17 May 1993, in author's collection.
39   Hans Decker. "Overview of Hutterite History," [ca. 1980s], in author's collection.

Ältester Jacob Kleinsasser (Crystal Spring, MB) and Jacob Hofer (Woodland, Manitoba) with Manitoba NDP Premier Edward Schreyer. [SOURCE: Jacob Kleinsasser Collection.]

were deemed of little worth in the workforce were appointed 'German' school teachers. This led to a sharp decline in the level of education offered to Hutterite children. According to Hans Decker, unhealthy competition began to develop between wealthier communities and poorer communities as the poorer communities tried to match the living standards of their wealthier counterparts. This high standard of living saw communities build unnecessarily large housing units and purchase the best vehicles and trucks available on the market.[40]

In the early 1980s, a recession hit North America, causing the Hutterites to experience high inflation and interest rates. The Bank of Canada's interest rate hit 21% in August of 1981, and the inflation rate averaged more than 12%. The Hutterite communities most affected by the recession were those which needed to finance the purchase of more land to establish daughter communities. In 1984 the *Ältester* and other ministers met with many bankers, stockbrokers, fund managers, and financial experts in an attempt to find

---

40 John [Hans] Decker, "*Herr Gott gib mi[r] Wahrheit…* [Lord God, give me the truth]," (9 April 1985), unpublished manuscript, in author's collection, 4–5.

The 1980s saw the establishment of the H. B. Mutual Insurance Company. The Hutterites, from left to right, are Jacob Hofer (Woodland), Jacob Kleinsasser (Crystal Spring), Edward Kleinsasser (Sunnyside), Mike Waldner (Milltown), Jacob Hofer (Valley View), and Jacob 'Uli' Waldner (Huron). [SOURCE: Jacob Kleinsasser Collection.]

answers to these challenges.[41] The new church organizations that were developed as part of this process of consultation needed financial commitments from the individual Schmiedeleut communities. For instance, when the church credit corporation was established, it was decided that the wealthier communities were to contribute $10,000 annually and the poorer communities $5,000. At the same time, a $1,000,000 loan was taken from the bank. As the communities' share of the contribution grew, the interest rate owing to the bank would become progressively less. For the most part, these financial manoeuvres were successful and in the long term benefited the overall church. However, it must also be acknowledged that they created a lot of tension and disunity. For instance, the fact that there was already an economic crisis meant that those communities struggling financially now had the extra burden of having to contribute funds to church organizations. Many community leaders considered these contributions to be an 'imposed tax' and found various ways to avoid paying their community's share. The issue of communities refusing to pay into joint church projects also

---

41 Michael F. C. Radcliffe to Jakob Kleinsasser, 22 September 1992, in author's collection.

has a long history. Even though the annual conference of stewards and ministers agreed that individual communities would lay aside funds to help financially struggling communities, some simply refused to comply.

By the early 1990s, the American and some Canadian Schmiedeleut communities began to withdraw from the church organizations without consent from the rest of the Manitoba communities. Tension within the Schmiedeleut Conference began to build as the Schmiedeleut *Ältester* soon found himself facing stronger criticism. Other major events taking place during this time generated an enormous amount of confusion and dissent. The Lakeside litigation, the Springhill abattoir levy, and a financial crisis involving two South Dakota Schmiedeleut communities soon led to open revolt. Whenever the Schmiedeleut ministers had a meeting, the *Ältester* faced a constant barrage of demands to explain the situation. However, his attempts to explain the complexity of what was taking place failed to silence the opposition.

Before he became *Ältester*, and during the first decade in office, Jacob Kleinsasser enjoyed a strong popularity rating. His negotiations with the provincial and federal governments on behalf of all Hutterites were seen by most as positive and necessary manoeuvres. However, when he pushed for social and ethical reforms and began establishing financial institutions to help struggling Schmiedeleut communities, his popularity quickly began to decline.

The multiple factors which ultimately led to the church schism of 1992, are far to complex too cover in this lecture. I wish to acknowledge that some might disagree with my assessment of it; indeed, I want to learn from that. We have all been shaped by the communities and people we grew up with. As such, we all experienced what happened in 1992 in different ways. Today is not the time or place where we can have an in-depth discussion about what happened in 1992. What everyone can agree on is that the deep disunity and animosity which developed within the Schmiedeleut Conference eventually led to one of the most painful schisms in Hutterite church history.

The 1992 Church Schism

The 1992 Schmiedeleut schism had at least three distinct phases. The initial phase involved growing disunity between the three Hutterite *Leut*. The locus of these tensions was the inter-*Leut* biennial meetings which were associated with the federally incorporated Hutterite Church in Canada. From its inception in the 1950s, the biennial meeting maintained a tenuous peace between the three groups. In the 1950s, the Hutterite church experienced outward pressure from individuals and the government for stricter land and taxation restrictions to curb the expansion of the Hutterite communities. However, by the late 1980s, many of these conflicts had been resolved and as a result, the latent internal issues, which had been set aside while the Hutterite communities fended off external attacks, began to re-emerge. One such issue was the conflict over income tax in which the Dariusleut leadership proposed amendments to the Hutterite constitution in an attempt to evade payment of income tax. The second and greater issue was the relationship with the Bruderhof. Ever since the uniting in 1974, the Darius- and Lehrerleut had become increasingly uncomfortable with the Bruderhof presence in the Hutterite Church. By 1987 they were demanding that the Bruderhof be removed. When it became clear that the Schmiedeleut would not excommunicate the Bruderhof, the Darius- and Lehrerleut drafted a letter in which they stated that they no longer recognized the Bruderhof as members of the Hutterian Brethren Church (an act which they formally carried out in 1990). The Schmiedeleut responded by refusing to attend the biennial conferences until the Darius- and the Lehrerleut retracted their statement. This was still the state of the relationship between the three groups in 1992.

The second phase of the schism was a series of meetings which took place in November of 1992 which were convened to address accusations brought against Jacob Kleinsasser. Joseph Wipf from Plainview, SD, acting as spokesmen for the American communities, read a letter of accusation against the *Ältester*. The meetings were concluded by 49 American ministers signing their name in support of this letter. On the 1st of December, a number of these American ministers attended a meeting with Darius- and Lehrerleut leaders in Springwater, Montana where they requested and were given a letter of support signed by both conference leaders against the leadership of Jacob Kleinsasser.

The final phase took place on the 9th of December at Starlite Community, MB. At this meeting, a letter of twelve allegations against the *Ältester* was read.[42] At this point, many ministers from the Manitoba Schmiedeleut group also stood in support of the 12-point letter drafted by the American communities. The specific details of this meeting and the resulting schism will not be covered in this lecture as they are far too complex to be treated fairly in the time remaining. Let it suffice to say that, as a result of this meeting, the Schmiedeleut conference split into two separate conferences. From 1992 to 2000, the two Schmiedeleut Conferences engaged in a bitter struggle to determine which group represented the authentic Schmiedeleut Hutterite Conference.

Even though the December 1, 1992 meeting is considered to be the official date of the schism, the actual parting of ways happened gradually over the next few months and even years. As the repercussions of what happened rippled through the Schmiedeleut, lines were formed—communities, families and loved ones were torn apart. In contrast to our foreparents' time, where it was persecution from outside the church that brought great hardship and pain, here the words of Canadian author Frank Steele, written in 1941, seemed to come true: "Someday there may come disintegration from within."[43]

Further Division

In 1993, the dissenting group of Schmiedeleut together with the Darius- and Lehrerleut drafted what became known as the 1993 Constitution[44] and asked all Hutterite communities to affirm it. Those Schmiedeleut who stayed loyal to Jacob Kleinsasser refused to affirm and instead chose to stay with the 1950s Constitution.[45]

---

42 Joseph Wipf to "*Liebe* [sic] *Brüder* [Dear Brothers," i.e., all Schmiedeleut ministers], 29 August 1992, in author's collection.
43 C. Frank Steele, "Canada's Hutterite Settlement," 314.
44 This event was triggered by the Vital Statistics naming dispute.
45 The new constitution came about due to a fight over who represented the actual Hutterite church.

This led to two years of legal skirmishes which served to entrench both sides in their position. At the same time, both sides were upset at the direction the whole conflict was going. A peaceful settlement seemed impossible while individual communities were still being torn apart, and close to a dozen lawsuits, pitting one Schmiedeleut group against the other, were still before the courts. Even the Darius- and Lehrerleut were becoming increasingly uncomfortable with the direction in which they saw the two Schmiedeleut groups heading. At a meeting in Rosetown, Saskatchewan, they counselled the Group II leadership to do whatever they could to put an end to this church war. Eventually renewed efforts at finding a peaceful solution brought about a landmark written agreement in which both sides agreed to cancel immediately all legal challenges and work towards a peaceful division of the contested Schmiedeleut communities.[46]

The May 1995 agreement brought about an important but fragile peace. What it demonstrated was that there were parties on all sides who wanted to resolve the conflict peacefully, but relationships between the individuals brokering the peace deal and the two groups were so severely damaged, that the agreement had a tenuous foundation at best. Despite this, the May agreement did achieve its primary objectives.

For the most part, the contested Schmiedeleut communities were divided on a *pro rata* basis thus avoiding costly litigation. However, in some of the contested communities, the animosity and distrust were so deep-rooted that the agreement broke. In three of these communities—Oakbluff/Prairie Blossom, Cypress/MillsHof, and Sprucewood/Fairway—major disagreements erupted about the value of the assets which were to be divided. In the end, both groups bitterly accused each other of violating and breaking the agreement, and so the proverbial trenches were dug deeper as both sides refused to compromise their positions to reach a consensus.

From 1996 to 2000 the two Schmiedeleut Conferences were again on the verge of a costly and lengthy legal battle. Even though the two groups had agreed, in principle, to recognize each other, a legal

---

46 "Agreement between Manitoba Schmiedeleut Group One and Two," 2 May 1995, in author's collection.

Letter of Understanding

April 10, 2000

The Hutterian Brethren Church consists of 3 conferences:
Dariusleut Lehrerleut Schmiedeleut

The Schmiedeleut conference consists of 2 groups.

Both groups of the Schmiedeleut conference are in agreement that the Schmiedeleut Conference will live under the umbrella of the Hutterian Brethren Church,

Neither group wishes to pursue either group in the courts, they both wish to" continue on as Hutterian Brethren and desire to live harmoniously with each other within the Hutterian Brethren Church.

This understanding replaces all prior statements and is made as a result of a -desire by the 2 groups of the Schmiedleut Conference of the Hutterian Brethren Church to put to rest their disputes regarding their names and status.

[signatures: Michael Hofer, S Waldner, Leonard Kleinsasser, Mike Waldner]

The Letter of Understanding from April 2000 represented a ceasefire that enabled both groups to co-exist under the Hutterite banner without further litigation. Signatories are Michael Hofer (Sommerfeld, Group II), Samuel Waldner (Decker, Group I), Leonard Kleinsasser (Delta, Group II), and Mike Waldner (Rosedale, Group I). [SOURCE: Author's collection.]

battle over who possessed the rights to the name Schmiedeleut and Hutterian Brethren was about to be fought out in the Canadian courts. Again, both sides realized that they did not want this conflict to escalate and both sides agreed to meet to work out a peaceful solution. Samuel Waldner from Decker community summarized what many felt: "It is high time to stop putting up walls and time to start building bridges instead. It is time that we start acting like the Christians that we claim to be."[47]

---

47 Samuel Waldner. "Compilation of Minutes of Group I and II Uniting Talks," 3 March 2000, in author's collection.

On April 10, 2000, leaders from both Schmiedeleut conferences met in Winnipeg and drafted a Letter of Understanding in which both groups agreed to share the name Hutterian Brethren Church and that they had a "desire to live harmoniously with each other within the Hutterian Brethren Church."[48] The two groups subsequently adopted the names Group I, Hutterian Brethren Church 1950 Constitution, and Group II, Hutterian Brethren Church 1993 Constitution.

Concluding Thoughts

The last three decades have been years of disunity, years of wounding, and years of deep pain for many Hutterites. In this time, numerous attempts were made to heal the schism and to establish peaceful relations, but most have failed. However, there are reasons to be hopeful. There are many Hutterites on both sides of this unfortunate division who are actively and courageously seeking ways toward forgiveness and reconciliation. This work will need to be undertaken with sensitivity so as not to deepen old wounds and inflame grievances. As we continue this journey of healing, we all need to cloak ourselves with the humility of Christ so that we can confess our personal and collective sins of disunity, strife, and pride which have torn deeply into the fabric of our existence as a people of God.

When we look back at the last one hundred years, we can see how the Hutterite Church has evolved. Change came about through our interaction with other communal groups such as the Harmonists in Pennsylvania, the Amana communities of Iowa, and the Bruderhof communities. At the same time, many changes came about simply because of the progression of time, the modernization of our world, and conflicts with our host society. In recent decades, many changes came about because of internal conflict as the different *Leut* struggled with competing visions of what it meant to be a Hutterite. Ever since arriving in North America, the Hutterites have been divided into three conferences which have each evolved their own identity. After 1918 the Hutterites became further divided into American and Canadian communities. One can observe

---

48   "Letter of Understanding," 10 April 2000, in author's collection.

fundamental differences between the various *Leut* which stem from their national identity.

When the Schmiedeleut Conference experienced a painful schism in 1992, two different groups of Schmiedeleut came into existence. Significant ideological differences developed between these two groups as they struggled to form their own identities. Intermarriage between the two groups never ceased but remained a constant source of tension.

The mid-1990s saw the Hutterites again part ways with the Bruderhof communities. They have developed their own identity. At the same time, because of our shared history and intermarriages, there is still a bond between the two groups. In the late 1990s, there was also the emergence of independent Hutterite communities such as Fort Pitt in Saskatchewan, and Altona, Elmendorf, and Grand River in the USA. What implications these developments will have on the overall Hutterite world remains unclear. The initial response within the Hutterite community to these developments was to launch the *Meidung* or the banning wars. However, the *Meidung* proved to be extremely unpopular within the larger Hutterite congregational context. Certain leaders pushed for the establishment of boundaries, as they saw the issue as a deeply spiritual issue. When we look back on this process, it becomes evident that most Hutterite members never fully accepted *Meidung* as many felt they had little or no voice in the decision. Part of our present-day reality is that we have created an ethical dualism in which each group sees itself as the 'pure' Hutterite church, and the others, if not decidedly evil, at the very least, second class. This kind of thinking is crippling and wounding, making it almost impossible to seek reconciliation. Ethical dualism leads to the establishment of walls. It sees the world as black and white, right or wrong. There is no middle ground. As a Christian people, we are called to be kind and tolerant to each other.

I want to conclude by reflecting on the legacy of my grandfather, Jacob Maendel whose vision for community life, his love for nature, laughter, and story had the ability to inspire others.

Jacob Maendel's spirit of openness inspired a number of non-Hutterites to visit his community of New Rosedale, in an effort to explore communal living: John Gabor, John Szüsz, Elmer Baer and Norman Randall, as well as the families of Allan and Sylvester Baer, Christian Dornn and Alexander Georg. Most of them were immigrants to Canada—Gabor and Szüsz from Hungary, Randall from England, the Dornns from Russia, the Georgs from Germany, and the Baers from Ontario.

However, Jacob's story is not just his own. Like many of us, he stood on the shoulders of others whose vision of compassion and helping others, inspired and shaped his life. One such person was Jacob's father, Joseph Maendel. Born in the US, Joseph served as *Haushalter* in Rosedale Community, Elie, MB, where he became acquainted with the Métis people of St. Eustache, just across the river from Rosedale. "These Métis do not fit in with the larger society," he commented. "They are like us in that respect, so it is fitting and right for us to help and support them."[49] The Rosedale *Buebm* played hockey on the river with their Métis neighbours, learning each other's language in the process. Joseph Maendel welcomed his Métis neighbours into his home and community. One senior man spent countless evenings in the Maendel home, where visitors were treated like members of the family. During the difficult years of the Great Depression, various St. Eustache folk regularly enjoyed a meal in the Rosedale communal dining hall and usually left with extra food to take home.[50]

The stories of Joseph and Jacob Maendel challenge us to share our homes, our resources, and our communities with our neighbours. It is their witness to a spirit of openness and acceptance of others which may provide us with a way forward in our struggle to find peace and unity among ourselves and with others. In the words of Jean Vanier, the late Canadian humanitarian and founder of the L'Arche communities,

> to work for peace in community, through acceptance of others as they are, and through constant forgiveness, is to work for peace in the world and

---

49 Dora Maendel to Ian Kleinsasser, 29 May 2019, in author's collection.
50 Ibid.

for true political solutions; it is to work for the Kingdom of God.[51]

---

51 Jean Vanier, *Community and Growth* (London: Darton, Longman and Todd, 1989), 100.

About Jacob D. Maendel
(1911–1972)

Jacob D. Maendel was a Hutterite teacher, pastor, and community leader. Born in 1911 at Rosedale Community near Alexandria, South Dakota, he migrated to Manitoba in 1918 when Hutterites fled political persecution because of their commitment to nonviolence. He was chosen as minister in 1949 at New Rosedale Community and went on to become widely regarded as a leader ahead of his time.

In an era when it was considered good economic sense to clear wooded land for use as fertile farmland, he insisted that strips of forest be conserved as ecological buffer zones. Both the task of selecting the site for a new community and the work of establishing Fairholme Community (1957–1959) were informed by his deep appreciation for nature: Jacob insisted on an acreage of bush above the Assiniboine River, and ensured that the natural environment remains as intact as possible, thereby gaining a reputation as "a staunch defender of trees."

Jacob Maendel also had an ecumenical vision. Although Hutterites of the mid-20th-century were characterized by exclusivism and sectarianism, Jacob was open to learning from non-Hutterites in a way that was enriching for the larger Hutterian Community. His outward-looking vision of faithful Christian discipleship led to newcomers—families as well as single adults—visiting New Rosedale: some stayed briefly, while others became permanent members.

Despite his basic grade seven education, he was a self-educated lifelong learner who read widely and introduced his students to great thinkers like Dietrich Bonhoeffer, Sigmund Freud, Helen Keller, and John Milton. Maendel understood the value of a culturally sensitive education and his vision led to the teaching career of Peter Maendel—the first Hutterite to attend and graduate from the Manitoba Teacher's College. This resulted in the unique dynasty of Maendel educators among Manitoba Hutterites today.

Ultimately, Jacob's vision and focus were the impetus for a surge of interest in education among Schmiedeleut I Hutterites that has culminated in nearly 100 Hutterite teachers holding Arts and Education degrees and teaching Hutterite children in their respective communities.

Jacob Maendel died in 1972. With gratitude to God for his work, witness, and inspiration, we name this lecture series in his honour.

About Ian Kleinsasser

Ian Kleinsasser is an independent researcher based out of Crystal Spring Hutterite Community near St. Agathe, MB. He holds a Bachelor of Arts and an Education after degree from Brandon University. Ian has given numerous presentations at the annual conference for Hutterite German teachers and the International Conference for Hutterite Educators. His groundbreaking article on the 1992 Schmiedeleut church schism will be published in *Navigating Tradition and Innovation* by the Hutterian Brethren Book Centre in 2019. Kleinsasser's research focuses primarily on the Hutterianism of the 19th and 20th centuries. He and his wife, Jolene, are parents of five lively children who are a constant reminder of why he pursues historical research. Jacob D. Maendel is his maternal grandfather.

www.ingramcontent.com/pod-product-compliance
Lightning Source LLC
Chambersburg PA
CBHW041129110526
44592CB00020B/2745